John Bunyan

PILGRIM AND DREAMER

(Ernest Wallace)

ERNEST W. BACON

BAKER BOOK HOUSE
Grand Rapids, Michigan 49506

Reprinted 1984 by Baker Book House
with permission of copyright owner
and The Paternoster Press

Formerly published under the title
Pilgrim and Dreamer

ISBN: 0-8010-0869-7

Printed in the United States of America

Contents

Dedicated to the memory of
DR ALEXANDER WHYTE
a great lover of John Bunyan
who led me into many of the deep things
of the spiritual life

Preface

It is some years since an adequate biography of John Bunyan has been issued. By adequate is meant one which is based on the latest historical research into the life of Bunyan and his times, and which in addition is true to the Evangelical and Puritan principles which, at such great cost, he upheld. This book claims to meet both these important requirements.

Books there are about John Bunyan, some admiring him, others critical of him. This raises the vital question of the relationship of the biographer to his subject. Should he be detached from his subject, or involved with him?

Obviously a biography of Bunyan by one who is strongly opposed to Puritanism, or who does not understand its distinctive principles, is unlikely to be successful. A book about the author of *The Pilgrim's Progress* written by one who is not himself a Christian pilgrim cannot be reliable. We have had writings by Anglo-Catholics and by secular psychiatrists to whom the mind and spirit of John Bunyan were completely alien. How could it be otherwise?

Ideally the writer on John Bunyan should be deeply involved with his subject, and yet at the same time, in some sense, detached from it. The present writer feels bound to "declare his interest". From college days when he first began to study Bunyan, he has learned to love and value his many works. He, too, has been led to hold Puritan principles and values as the best of the Puritans held them in the seventeenth century. There is a spiritual affinity with Bunyan, an agreement with him on all the chief points of doctrine and Church government. At the same time, the author is detached from the subject in so far as he surveys Bunyan's scene and activities from the point of view of a different century with a totally different ethos. Nor can one wholly endorse everything John Bunyan wrote, for though deeply taught of the Spirit he was still a child of his times.

At the same time, this great Englishman and Christian writer, who made such a great contribution to the spiritual knowledge and religious and civil liberties of his day, speaks to our age also. With all our scientific and technical knowledge, our landing on the moon and voyages in space, our vision of world unity and peace (still so far from being realised), we still need to know God and his saving grace, and how the burden of our sin and guilt can be lifted and how, at the last, we can enter with joy into the gate of the Celestial City. No knowledge is more vital than this.

This, John Bunyan can tell us, if only we will listen.

Appreciations

For valuable advice and suggestions at more than one stage in writing this work, I am most grateful to the following: Miss Hilary Platt B.A., Hon. Sec. of the Cromwell Association founded by Isaac Foot; the late Rev J.G.G. Norman M.Th; Rev Gilbert Kirby M.A.; Mr Thomas Harris; my Editor Mr P.E. Cousins of Paternoster Press; the librarians of the Public Libraries at Winscombe, Avon, and at Bath, Somerset; and doubtless to many others also.

There may well be errors of omission and commission to be discovered in this book, and these will be rectified if another edition is called for. The Lord has shown me that a book such as this can bring both blessing and salvation to many souls.

Ernest W. Bacon

1

Lowly Beginnings

John Bunyan was born at Elstow, near Bedford, sometime in the Autumn of 1628. The exact date is unknown, for compulsory registration of births did not begin until 1837, and at the time of Bunyan's birth parish registers were often very carelessly kept. His baptism in the Parish Church of Elstow is recorded, however. In the parish register the Rev. Thomas Kellie, Vicar of Elstow, recorded the christening thus:- "John, the sonne of Thomas Bonnionn Jun., the 30th of November, 1628." So John may have been born in October or November of that year. His parents were very proud of him, for he was a big strong child with lusty lungs, and a reddish tinge to the fair hair on his downy head.

1

In his autobiography, *Grace Abounding*, published in 1666, John Bunyan speaks of his ancestry thus: "My descent then, it was, as is well known by many, of a low and inconsiderable generation; my Father's house being of that rank that is meanest and most despised of all the families in the land." In this, it is clear, Bunyan spoke too disparagingly of his family. For, in fact, he came from an original Norman family that had possessed considerable land, but was by now in decline. He belonged to a family of Bedfordshire peasants whose genealogy has been traced back for many generations in local records. Although he did not know it his name was of aristocratic origin, from the Norman-French "Buignon", a bun or fruit pattie. An ancestor very probably came from Normandy soon after the Conquest, for there were Bunyans in north Bedfordshire as early as 1199. These early Bunyans possessed land, for in 1199 a certain William Buniun was involved in a lawsuit at the Court of King's Bench with the Abbess of Elstow concerning land that William held from William of Wilsamstede, but which was claimed by the Abbess. The precise amount of land possessed by this distant ancestor of John Bunyan is not known, but it is evident that during the intervening centuries most of it passed into the hands of neighbouring landowners and farmers. When John was born his father, Thomas Bunyan, owned a field still called "Bunyan's field", and also a large cornfield of several acres to the west of it. Indeed, as early as 1542 the Court Roll of the Manor described the eastern extremity of Elstow parish as "Bonyon's End". The family, therefore, for many generations were freehold landowners, but declined in status until they merged into peasant stock.

The surname Bunyan was variously spelt, and there are thirty-four variants of it found in ancient records, such as Buingnan, Binyan, Bonion Bonnion, Boynon, Bonyon, Bunyon. Bunyan, which has become universally accepted, is certainly the least frequent.

Little is known of John's grandparents. His grandfather, Thomas, describes himself in his will as a "pettie chapman" or small trader, most probably travelling through the neighbouring towns and villages selling domestic wares, and perhaps the ill-printed little books of romances and fairy-tales of those days.

Thomas Bunyan Junior, John's father, whose name written by the Elstow Vicar is given as Bonnionn, was born in February 1603. He was in fact a man of some considerable hereditary substance. He described himself as a "braseyer" or brazier, and was the first member of his family to follow this occupation. Early biographers of Bunyan, influenced by

Sir Walter Scott, mistakenly thought that John was of gipsy descent because his father was a "tinker", a mender of pots and pans. But there was no gipsy blood in John Bunyan. His father was more of a village blacksmith, although no doubt he travelled the nearby villages ready to mend kettles and grind scissors and knives. He had inherited not only nine acres of land in the hamlet of Harrowden, which marked the eastern end of Elstow parish, but also property in nearby Kempston. At the corner of one of his fields at Harrowden stood a small thatched cottage with an outbuilding which contained Thomas's forge and the implements of his trade. An old drawing shows it to have been a superior type of cottage with a window on each side of the front door, and no less than five windows on the first floor. It disappeared about 1840, but the site is known, marked by a weed-covered mound. From the meadow the Bunyans could see the distant tower and steeple of Elstow Church, and no doubt hear the bells, in which John was to find so much delight, ringing for worship. Thomas Bunyan, according to Charles Doe the Southwark comb-maker, who wrote a brief account of his hero John in 1692, was "of the national religion", i.e. Church of England, and a Royalist. Four years before the execution of Charles I Thomas named his third son Charles.

2

On May 23, 1627 Thomas Bunyan married Margaret Bentley at Elstow Church. Her mother, Mary Bentley who was a widow seems to have been comfortably off, occupying a well-equipped brick and timber cottage in Elstow village street. Margaret was 23 and Thomas 24. He was her first husband, but she was his second wife. He had been married at the age of twenty to Anne Pinney, who died childless in 1627 after four years of marriage. Quite soon afterwards Thomas married again. Margaret Bentley must have known Thomas Bunyan all her life, but, alas, we have no description or information concerning her. John, her firstborn, was born in the cottage at Harrowden; his sister Margaret some fifteen months after; and his brother William in 1635.

When Bunyan was born Shakespeare had been dead twelve years, but his fame was firmly established and his plays constantly performed. John Milton, whose "Paradise Lost" Bunyan may have read, was in his third year at Christ's College, Cambridge—the University that was to produce so many Puritan writers and leaders. At Oxford, Edward Hyde, later Lord Clarendon, had recently graduated from Magdalen College, and was preparing for a legal career at the Middle Temple, London. Under his legislation, the *Clarendon Code*, John was to be penalized and imprisoned. But his loving parents bringing him to the font in Elstow Church, had no thought of these great men of the future, or that their little John would, in many respects, be even more influential than they. 1628 was important in other ways, for it was the year of the Petition of Right, the death of Buckingham, and the entry into Parliament of Oliver Cromwell.

Elstow, by the time of John Bunyan's birth, was an old village which had once occupied a considerable place in history. In Domesday Book it is recorded as "Elnestou" which is a debased form of "Helenstow", meaning Helen's Place. The name is derived from the dedication of a very early church to Saint Helena, mother of the British born Roman Emperor, Constantine the Great, the first Christian ruler of that Empire. Helenstow, by the time of Bunyan's day, had been abbreviated to Elstow. Countess Judith, niece of William the Conqueror, had founded a Benedictine Convent there in 1078, and many supposed that whatever her past, the building was an attempt to quiet a most troubled conscience. Three years previously she had inadvertently betrayed her husband Waltheof, the Saxon Earl of Northampton, who had plotted against the conquering Normans.

The church where Bunyan was christened was originally the Abbey Church of the Benedictine Convent, which, for nearly five hundred years before the Dissolution of the Monasteries by Henry the Eighth in 1539, had exercised almost despotic power over the local inhabitants. The convent was severely censured by John Langland, Bishop of Lincoln in 1530 for lax discipline and neglect of religious services. The Abbey was dissolved in 1539, and the Abbess was pensioned off at £50 per annum, and the nuns at £2 per annum. The Abbey was granted in 1553 to Sir Humphrey Ratcliffe, who used much of the stone of the convent's domestic buildings to build himself a mansion nearby. Next came Sir Thomas Hillersdon who, in the reign of Charles I, replaced Ratcliffe's house with a stately Renaissance style mansion named Elstow Place, said to have been designed by Inigo Jones. The ruins of this building stand on the south side of the Church.

The Parish Church of Elstow is only the nave of the Abbey Church, a building of unusual loftiness and dignity, of the Norman and Early English periods, with fine well-proportioned arches. In 1580 the old tower and chancel were demolished, and the flanking tower of the nunnery, a massive and strongly buttressed structure, separated from the body of the church by several yards, was enlarged to contain the bells. This is the "steeple house" which was the scene of Bunyan's bell-ringing. The truncated church, never joined to the new steeple, became the parish church of Elstow, dedicated to the Holy Trinity. The octagonal font, in which John Bunyan and his first two children were baptised, is still to be seen although not in use. The pentagonal pulpit, from which Christopher Hall preached the sermons that so impressed John, also survives.

3

Elstow, although Bedford has spread out towards it, is still a very pleasant place, largely because of the widespreading village green situated quite near to the Church. Henry II had granted the right of holding annual fairs on the green in May and November. These provided an opportunity for cheap-jacks to sell their wares, but also for a variety of entertainers to perform, such as jugglers, morris-dancers, clowns, acrobats and strolling players. No doubt when Bunyan came to describe "Vanity Fair" in *The Pilgrim's Progress* he recalled the days of his youth at Elstow fairs. Horse fairs and cattle fairs were also held on the green.

At the eastern end of the village green stood the ancient Moot Hall, a barn-like structure of brick and timber with large gable ends, the upper storey slightly projecting above the ground floor. It is said to be of Saxon origin, and it is decorated with curious carvings dating from the fifteenth century. The lower part had consisted of shops at a former period, but even in Bunyan's day the upper part was used for village dances and other social occasions. Its chief use, however, was as a Court of Justice where magistrates settled disputes and tried petty offenders. To the west of the Moot Hall stood the grey stone market cross to be associated in years to come with John's conversion.

On three sides of the village green stand brick and timber cottages in a variety of shapes and sizes, with overhanging storeys and gabled porches, very picturesque, but modernized in more recent years. They must be much the same as in the days of the Commonwealth. The main village street is linked to the village green by a narrow lane. In the main part of the village were cottages and small houses, sundry shops, and two inns, the Red Lion and the Swan. But the meadows and woods and streams were only a short distance from the village in John's time, and as a country lad he would soon have become familiar with the birds, insects and farm animals of his day. No doubt, as was customary then, he would join the villagers working in the fields during haytime and harvest. Even today, when industrial development and town planning have crept up to and over Elstow, the citizens of Bedford can reach beautiful open countryside in ten minutes' walking.

Village life at Elstow in Bunyan's day was very different from the domestic and social life of the countryside today. Then the men toiled in the fields for low wages, or worked as cowmen, carpenters, shepherds, hostlers etc. The women did not go out to work as they do today; they had plenty to do even in the smallest house, with baking, making the family clothes, tending the chickens, and bringing up the children. Thomas Bunyan most likely grazed a cow or a couple of pigs on the field where his cottage stood and grew corn on his adjoining land. Of social life there was little, except that which the inns could afford, the occasional village dance at the Moot Hall, and the annual fairs. The Sunday services at the Church, attendance at which was compulsory by law, and the local weddings and funerals, also provided opportunities for village folk to get together.

4

Although his parents were comparatively poor (though Thomas Bunyan must have made a sufficient income from his tinkering for his small family), they were determined to send their son John to school. In *Grace Abounding* he says, "It pleased God to put into their hearts to put me to school both to read and write." He adds, "The which also I attained, according to the rate of other poor men's children; though to my shame I confess I did soon lose that little I learnt, even almost utterly." It is not known to which school he was sent, but there were two possibilities. There was the Grammar School at Bedford, founded by Sir William Harper who was born at Bedford in 1496. Moving to London he became a wealthy merchant and member of the Merchant Taylors' Company. In 1561 he became Lord Mayor of London and was knighted. Five years later he bought property in Holborn with which to endow a Grammar School in his native Bedford. By Bunyan's time, however, the school thus founded was in difficulties, and when he was between nine and twelve years of age, complaints were made against the schoolmaster, William Varney, that he not only charged fees which he had no right to do, but also grossly neglected the school by frequent absences from it, by spending a good deal of time in ale-houses, and was somewhat cruel in his discipline of the boys. It is probable that John sat at the battered, ink-stained, knife-carved desks of this school, where he learned not only to read and write, but also a smattering of Latin and Greek, for he uses several Latin and Greek words in his books.

Alternatively John Bunyan may have attended the Free School in the neighbouring parish of Houghton Conquest, established by Sir Francis Clarke. This school was under the control of Sidney Sussex College, Cambridge, but by 1645, later of course than Bunyan's brief schooldays, it also had fallen on evil times, its master Christopher Hills being dismissed for the wilful neglect of his duties. Educational establishments in those days were often far from satisfactory.

At whichever school he attended John did learn reading and writing, and despite his own statement it is most probably that he retained these elementary skills, though other subjects were largely forgotten. "The education he received," remarks Dr John Brown, "was mainly that given in the great school of human life where so many other sturdy natures have received such effective training." In the cottage where he was born would have been a copy of the Authorised Version of the Bible published in 1611, and no doubt this was read by his parents and sometimes by John himself.

"I never went to school to Plato or Aristotle," he was to write, "but was brought up at my father's house in a very mean condition, among a company of poor countrymen." He was set to work early at his father's smithy, apprenticed to his father's craft of brazier, learning how to use the forge, and to handle the anvil and the other tools of the trade. As a strong lad and willing to learn he soon made headway in the craft of mending household implements and the making and mending of cart-wheels and iron gates. One unfortunate habit he seems to have learned from his father was that of cursing and swearing, which persisted until his conversion. There is little doubt that swearing is a habit of those of very limited vocabulary, which Thomas Bunyan the father, being little educated himself would naturally indulge in. Bunyan says that he had few equals, even when a child, for cursing, swearing, lying and blaspheming the name of God. The grace of God was to cure him of all these in due time.

One childhood characteristic which never left him was a vivid and active imagination, to be transformed and sanctified and "made meet for the Master's use". He tells us in *Grace Abounding* that as a child of ten years he was frightened by fearful dreams and terrified by dreadful visions. He imagined with vivid clearness the devil and wicked spirits. He was also troubled with thoughts of the Day of Judgement and the doom of the ungodly in hell fire. He wondered whether it would be his lot to join them! He tells us that until he married he was the ring-leader of all the village youth in "all manner of vice and un-godliness". We shall examine in a later chapter the exact meaning of these words. Coleridge describes him at this stage as "a bitter black-guard", and probably this is not far short of the truth.

Very few incidents of his early life have come down to us, but there are a few interesting glimpses which show us his enjoyment of an outdoor life. Once he came across an adder crossing the highroad, and with the utmost bravado stunned it with a stick, forced open its mouth with his fingers, and plucked out its sting. Another time he accompanied his father on a considerable river trip by barge from Bedford to King's Lynn, where Thomas imported metals for his trade. John had long been fascinated by the river Ouse and its traffic, and would spend hours watching the horse-drawn barges bringing bales of wool and huge baskets of fruit and vegetables inland. On the King's Lynn trip he fell into a creek of the sea and was half-drowned when rescued. This was one of several narrow escapes which in later years he saw as evidence of God's mercy. Like most country boys he was fond of fishing, and good at it. One afternoon with his sister Margaret he was in a boat on the deepest part of the Ouse near Bedford when, foolishly standing up, he over-balanced, and fell into the river, and managed only with difficulty to clamber back from the grasp of the clinging reeds.

Years later John was to recall his boyhood fishing trips in his poetic introduction to *The Pilgrim's Progress*:

> You see the ways the fisherman doth take
> To catch the fish; what engins doth he make?

Behold how he engageth all his wits,
Also his snares, lines, angels, hooks and nets.
Yet fish there be, that neither hook nor line,
Nor snare nor net nor engine can make thine;
They must be grop't for, and be tickled too,
Or they will not be catcht, what e're you do.

John also learned to ride a horse—probably his father grazed one of his own in the meadow. He and his father made journeys on horseback, John riding pillion, across the country when Thomas had to go farther afield for work. He soon came to know the surrounding villages and small towns, the roads with their waggons, coaches, flocks and herds, riders and foot-travellers. Thomas would point out to John the stately mansions of the rich to which he was sometimes summoned to work at his trade, and the extensive parks full of fine trees which surrounded them. He would also point out relics of earlier ages, the hut-circles of the ancient Britons, the hill-fortresses of the warring British tribes, and the Roman camps also in strategic positions on the hills.

In 1641 when John was twelve years old he was a witness of an event which made a small but significant contribution to the political and social disruption so soon to burst upon the country. On Tuesday, March 16th, Sir Roger Burgoyne, one of the four members of Parliament for the County of Bedfordshire, led a company of two thousand leading citizens of Bedford and other places to present a petition to the Long Parliament. This was only one of many carried to London from all parts of the country. It requested the displacement of evil councillors, the punishment of delinquents, and the removal of all burdensome and scandalous ceremonies in the Church, and of all corrupt and scandalous ministers. These requests referred particularly to the Earl of Strafford chief adviser to Charles I, and chiefly responsible for his arbitrary policy, and to Archbishop Laud, also a chief adviser to the king, and a vigorous persecutor of dissenters. Both men were prisoners in the Tower of London and both later executed.

Elstow being on the highroad to London, John and Margaret together with their six year old brother William, would have watched with excited interest the large company of petitioners riding on horseback, four abreast, with their "protestations" in their hats. It must have been a stirring sight. In the City of London the petitioners were greeted with enthusiasm by excited crowds who yelled for spiritual liberty against both clerics and courtiers. The petition was received with eager sympathy by the House of Commons, amongst them, John Hampden and Oliver Cromwell, in whom the Puritan spirit burned as an inextinguishable flame.

2

Puritan England

John Bunyan cannot be understood unless he is seen against the contemporary religious and historical background.

The Puritans have been, and still are in some quarters, the most maligned and misrepresented of men. The very word "Puritan" has become a term of scorn, implying a gloomy fanaticism, a narrow-minded bigotry, a blight on all that is free and joyous. Nothing is farther from the actual truth. In fact the Puritans were a body of men of God who brought a spiritual light to England, drew the nation back to moral values, and stamped a moral greatness upon her that no other group, religious or secular, has ever done. The hatred of the Puritans was deliberately fostered by their political and ecclesiastical enemies in the reign of Charles II, many of whom were avowed enemies of truth and godliness, or, like Edward Hyde, Earl of Clarendon, singularly blind to their real aims and principles, and wilfully opposed to anything they stood for be it good or bad.

1

Thomas Fuller in his *Church History of Great Britain* written in 1655, says the word "Puritan" came into use in 1564 when conformity in liturgy and ceremonial were being enforced. "Such as refused the same were branded with the odious name of Puritans ... But prophane mouths quickly improved this nickname, therewith on every occasion to abuse pious people, some of them so far from opposing the Liturgy that they endeavoured (according to the instructions thereof in the preparation to the Confession) to accompany the Minister with a pure heart and laboured (as it is in the Absolution) for a life pure and holy."

In his autobiography Richard Baxter, the eminent Puritan divine and scholar, records how his father, a strict Church of England man, was jeered at as a Puritan because he read the Bible on Sunday afternoons. The family was living in a Shropshire village in 1630 when Baxter was a boy. "When I heard them speak scornfully of others as Puritans whom I never knew, I was at first apt to believe all the lies and slanders wherewith they loaded them. But when I heard my own father so reproached, and perceived the drunkards were the forwardest in the reproach, I perceived that it was mere malice. For my father never scrupled Common Prayer or Ceremonies, nor spake against bishops, nor ever so much as prayed but by a Book or form, being not then acquainted with any that did otherwise. But only for reading Scripture when the rest were dancing on the Lord's Day, and for praying (by a form out of the Common Prayer Book) in his house, and for reproving drunkards and swearers, and for talking sometimes a few words of Scripture and the Life to come, he was reviled commonly by the name of Puritan, Precisian, and Hypocrite: and so were the godly conformable Ministers that lived anywhere in the country near us, not only by our neighbours, but by the common talk of the vulgar rabble all around us."

"The word 'Puritan'," says Dr Hugh Martin, "was apt to be used very vaguely and was found to be a useful term of abuse by those who disliked any stress on a moral life. Wycliffe and his Lollards were fore-runners of Puritanism, as were Hooper and Latimer: indeed the title might fairly be applied to the Wesleys and Whitefield and their fellow-labourers in the Evangelical Revival."

Puritanism began as a reform movement in the Church of England by men who desired the Reformation to be furthered in a purer and more scriptural direction. The Elizabethan Settlement in religion was an uneasy compromise between what we may call the Catholic and Protestant points of view. It retained elements from Medieval Catholicism but made concessions to those who desired to purge the Church from continuing Roman practices or tendencies. Above all the Puritans desired simpler and godly ministers who preached the great vital truths of the Word of God. Elizabeth I was in many ways a wise ruler but she lived in an era when monarchy was thorough-going dictatorship. Her oppressive Church policy not only forced Puritanism to become a reform movement within the Established Church, but drove large numbers of Puritans into separatist religious and political groups. Her ecclesiastical policy sowed the seeds of the Civil War. Her first Parliament passed two great Acts that had important and disastrous consequences. The Act of Supremacy declared that she was Supreme Governor in all spiritual and ecclesiastical affairs, as well as in temporal affairs. She used this power relentlessly, dragooning Archbishops and Bishops, and laying down the law herself in matters of theology, worship and vestments. The Act of Uniformity imposed severe penalties on any Minister who deviated from the Prayer Book services, and fines on those who deliberately absented themselves from divine service in the Parish Church. Bunyan was to feel the full power of this law in days to come. The Queen herself ordered that the surplice and cope and other Roman Catholic vestments were to be used in the service of Holy Communion. Trouble inevitably followed, for many clergy felt that they could not conscientiously wear vestments associated with the Roman Catholic mass which they abhorred. James I followed Elizabeth, and distinguished himself by the threatening remark about Nonconformists, "I will make them conform or harry them out of the land."

2

In 1572 the Puritan leaders drew up the "Admonition", a vigorous statement of the Puritan position. They protested that many ministers had no true call from God and were ignorant and inefficient, and that they administered the sacraments laxly. True Reformation, they urged, consisted in "abandoning all popish remnants both in ceremonies and regiment," and also "in bringing in and placing in God's Church those things only which the Lord Himself in His Word commandeth." They objected to the surplice because it was the priestly garment of pre-Reformation days, and preferred the black Geneva gown to which many of them had become accustomed when they were in exile in the persecuting days of Mary. They regarded the use of the sign of the cross in baptism as superstitious. They rejected kneeling at the Lord's Supper as implying adoration of the elements of bread and wine, and because Jesus and his disciples sat at the meal in the Upper Room. They also protested against certain festivals as being of pagan or Romish origin. It is interesting to note that in 1563 proposals along these lines had been brought before Convocation, and rejected by one vote only, 58 for the motion and 59 against. This indicates how evenly balanced the parties were in the Church of England at that time. But had the voting gone in favour of the Puritans, it is exceedingly unlikely that Queen Elizabeth would have accepted the proposed reforms. In 1566 Archbishop Parker summoned the London clergy to Lambeth Palace and demanded there and then a promise from each to wear the prescribed vestments. There were 110 ministers present, of whom 37 refused to conform. The minority, Parker reported to Cecil, "were the best." The nonconformists were suspended from all ministry: some became chaplains to Puritan gentry, some joined the Presbyterian Church of Scotland, some turned to the study of medicine, and some emigrated. Five remained undeterred, continued to minister, and were imprisoned.

The dominant aim of the Puritans as expressed in the "Admonition" was to purge the services of worship from all remnants of Romish teaching, practice, and superstition, and to procure in every parish an earnest, spiritually-minded, preaching minister. Their principles were rejected. The proposals enraged the Queen. She suspected the political tendencies of Puritanism, for it implied a threat to the royal supremacy in the Church. In a speech to Parliament at the beginning of the war with Spain she made her position clear, denouncing both Romanists and Puritans. "I mean to guide them both by God's holy true rule. In both parts be perils, and of the latter (i.e. Puritans) I must pronounce them dangerous to a kingly rule, to have every man according to his own censure to make a doom of the validity and privity of his Prince's government with a common vail and cover of God's Word." The early Puritans were far from any such intention. Cartright and Travers maintained that magistrates and princes were under the discipline of the Church in spiritual matters, like anyone else, but they had no political aims and repudiated any charge of disloyalty to the Crown.

The deplorable state of the Church in general in those days is now admitted on clear evidence. Non-residence of the clergy in their parishes from which they drew the income, and the holding of several livings and ecclesiastical offices in plurality, were very common. Large numbers of parishes had no adequate pastoral care. A survey in 1586 found only 2000 preachers in 10,000 parishes. Many parsons were ignorant men, others immoral, some chiefly taken up with hunting and other field sports. Archbishop Grindal of York in 1570, and of Canterbury in 1575 was sympathetic with much in the Puritan emphasis and outlook, and anxious to deal with abuses in the Church. He stoutly defended his efforts to secure and install godly preachers, and refused to suppress various Puritan meetings for Bible study and prayer. As a consequence, the Queen on her own authority suspended him from his duties for the last seven years of his life, although he nominally remained in office. He was undoubtedly a Puritan at heart. Whitgift, who succeeded Grindal, was of an entirely different outlook, was in full agreement with the Queen's opposition to all Puritan ideas, and vigorously enforced the regulations with great harshness. He it was who instituted the iniquitous Court of High Commission, which attained such shameful eminence under Archbishop Laud, and where men could be, and were, thrown into prison for some ecclesiastical offence without warrant and without trial.

3

There was an underlying unity of spiritual purpose among the various groups of Puritans. These were mainly: those who remained within the Anglican Church as true Evangelical Protestants, Presbyterians, Independents (or Congregationalist), and Baptists (at first and for many years called "Anabaptists", i.e. those who re-baptised after infancy). In addition there was the Society of Friends, contemptuously called "Quakers", and various sects such as Ranters, Fifth Monarchy men, and others.

Sufficient has perhaps been said of the conforming Puritans within the Church of England. Despite episcopal opposition and stiff laws and penalties, these Puritans remained active, chiefly amongst the laity and included many gentry and landowners. They never died out in the State Church and became the ancestors of the Evangelical party in the Church of England today.

The English Presbyterians, often in alliance with the Church of Scotland, desired a church founded on the Geneva model of Calvin. They were the dominant party in the Long Parliament, 1640-51, and the Westminster Assembly of Divines, 1643-49. They believed in the parity of ministers, denying any superior rank of bishops because in the New Testament presbyter and bishop are translations of the same Greek word. They believed strongly in the priesthood of all believers, the central doctrine of the Reformation, as did other Puritans. They believed in a graded system of church courts, in the grouping of local churches in presbyteries, with the associated presbyteries joined in synods, and a General Assembly made up of both ministers and lay elders as the supreme Church authority. John Geree in *The Character of an Old English Puritane* (1646), puts it thus: "They held God's rule for His Church Aristocratical by Elders, not Monarchical by Bishops, nor Democratical by the People." They believed that this form of Church government was to be found in Scripture. They not only objected to the rule of bishops, but also repudiated worship according to the Book of Common Prayer. The Westminster Assembly published a Directory of Worship which advocated extempore prayer. Dr Thomas Cartwright, the leading Puritan of the day, and Professor of Divinity at Cambridge until his ejection in 1570 was a Presbyterian. He taught Calvinist doctrine to some hundreds of students and his influence on them was far-reaching. Many of the nobility, country gentry and city merchants were Presbyterians. The leading doctrines of Presbyterianism are Calvinistic and Evangelical, and are enshrined in the Westminster Confession and the Longer and Shorter Catechisms. Presbyterians considered themselves as standing midway between the Episcopal Church and the Independent Sects. In 1572 a presbytery was set up in Wandsworth and in several other places. Cartwright and his fellow Puritans opposed separation from the Church of England in the hope that the Government would reform it in Puritan and Presbyterian directions. But it was a vain hope, and Presbyterian Puritanism never became a great force in England.

At first, and for some considerable time, the Independents included those we would now call Congregationalists and Baptists. But the distinctive position of the latter on the baptism of believers only led them to become a separate body in the course of time. There was an Independent congregation in London as early as 1571. The best known of their early leaders was Robert Browne who wrote a book that had a far-reaching influence entitled, *A Treatise of Reformation without Tarrying for Any*. He had been a student at Cambridge under Cartwright. According to Browne, the only Church is a local body of believers in Christ who voluntarily covenant together to live according to the law of God and of Christ; such a Church has Christ as its immediate Head, is self-governing by the appointment of elders and deacons, and chooses its own Pastor. When such a "gathered church" of believers met the Holy Spirit was considered to be in control, and the Church's activities to be guided by him. Browne founded a Congregational Church in Norwich in 1581, but because of much persecution and imprisonment he and the majority of his congregation sought refuge in Holland. Strangely enough, Browne himself later repudiated Independency and returned to the Church of England. Two other prominent leaders of the Independents were Greenwood and Barrow, associated with a church at Islington in 1586. They were imprisoned and executed at Tyburn in 1593. As a result of continued persecution of Independents under the Conventicle Act of 1593, many emigrated to Holland to seek liberty of worship denied them in England. It was exiles from Lincolnshire who formed the Church at Leyden from which the Pilgrim Fathers sailed in the Mayflower in 1620 to found New England. The Pastor of this Church was John Robinson, a learned and broad-minded man who asserted that "God has still more light and truth to shed forth from His Word." The leading personality amongst the Independents of the Commonwealth period was Dr John Owen. Originally a Presbyterian he changed to Independency, and was Dean of Christ Church, Oxford. His books are amongst the classics of Puritanism. He was the friend and chaplain to Oliver Cromwell, and strangely enough he was also the friend of Charles II, and spoke warmly to that monarch in praise of John Bunyan, the tinker of Bedford.

The Baptists were generally called "Anabaptists" by their opponents, because they re-baptised believers in adult years. But the term "anabaptist" linked them with those of that name whose fanatic excesses at Münster and elsewhere on the Continent brought them and their ideas into great disrepute. Baptists and Independents held identical views concerning the government and ordering of the church. They differed in that Baptists held that Christian baptism was the baptism of believers and not of infants. At first they baptised by affusion or pouring, but gradually they came to adopt immersion, although the mode of baptism was always of secondary importance to them. There were two parties amongst the Baptist sect. The General Baptists, under such leaders as Smyth and Helwys held Arminian views, i.e. that salvation was available to all, and that man, in some sense, could aid his own salvation. The Particular Baptists, originating in Jacob's Independent Church in London in 1616, were strongly Calvinistic, believing in "particular redemption", i.e. redemption for the elect only. Both sections grew steadily and John Bunyan entered into controversy with them as we shall see in a later chapter. It is often claimed that Bunyan himself was a Baptist but we shall see in due course that this is very uncertain. In Bedfordshire and some other places Independents and Baptists joined together in fellowship to found local churches, later called "Union Churches", and it was to one of these that Bunyan belonged.

The Quakers also formed one of the Puritan groups, although in the seventeenth century with their fanatical zeal, strange doctrines, and bizarre practices, they were far removed from "The Society of Friends" which today is renowned for its philanthropic and social work. Their doctrine of the "inner light" which all might develop to become mature Christians conflicted with the Calvinist doctrine of the fall of man and his total depravity. Their practice of waiting on God in silence for the Spirit to move them, and their apparent indifference to the use and authority of the Bible, raised up against them many opponents including John Bunyan and Richard Baxter. George Fox, 1624-90, the founder of the sect was a fiery prophet of a section of Puritanism, which denounced formal worship, a paid ministry, the taking of oaths, the removal of the hat as a mark of respect, and insisted on passive resistance to enemies. Cromwell endured much trouble from them, although conferring with George Fox brought him to a better understanding of them.

The extreme left-wing of the Puritan movement was occupied by small sects under such names as Levellers, Diggers, and Fifth Monarchy men. Though these groups had a religious origin they soon became radical sects with political and social reformist aims. They were in revolt against the whole established order of things, property, education, the Church, the franchise system, and much else. The Levellers' leader was John Lilburne, who demanded democracy based on Christian equality, and universal male suffrage. The Digger movement was confined to agricultural workers. Its leader, Gerard Winstanley, was a visionary. He wished to abolish money and commerce, and establish small, self-supporting communes. The Fifth Monarchy sect, or Millenarians, held that the four world empires of chapter seven of the Book of Daniel were coming to a close with the Protectorate of Cromwell. They looked for the immediate second coming of Christ to earth to set up his kingdom, the Fifth Monarchy. Some were peaceful though misguided Christians, but others became violent revolutionaries who had to be put down with bloodshed after the Restoration in 1661. They were to have a strong, indirect bearing on the course of John Bunyan's life.

4

Although in many matters there was a variety of view within the Puritan movement, there was an underlying unity on fundamental principles.

First, they held strongly to the Protestant emphasis on the Bible as the only rule of faith and conduct. (The Quakers alone were an exception to this). J. R. Green the historian says: "England became the people of a book, and that book was the Bible." It was, he adds, the one book that was familiar to every Englishman: it was read in churches and at home, and came to exercise a profound influence on thought, aims religious social and political, and on private conduct. The Puritans, following John Calvin, held that the Bible was authoritative for doctrine, forms of worship, and church government. The Authorised Version of 1611 was the chief literature for most people at a time when there were few other books or newspapers to distract their attention. It was read with simple belief in its literalness and infallibility. As John Bunyan shows in *Grace Abounding* the Bible was alternatively a source of comfort and torment. Cromwell found in the Bible abundance of texts to support his policies and adorn his letters and speeches. The words of Scripture became part of the common speech. Cromwell and other Puritan leaders did not use it merely to impress an audience; he used it to his wife, in letters to his friends, in Parliamentary speeches and army despatches. The Westminster Confession states that "our full persuasion and assurance of the infallible truth and divine authority (of the Bible) is from the inward work of the Holy Spirit, bearing witness by and with the Word in our hearts." The Puritan was certain that Scripture was more than an external authority; it was confirmed by the Spirit-prompted response of his mind and heart to the Word. To him, his authority was no longer an infallible Church or bishop or government, it was the Word of God, giving light on all points and in all circumstances. "Elizabeth," says J. R. Green, "might silence or tune the pulpits; but it was impossible for her to silence or tune the great preachers of justice and mercy and truth, who spoke from the Book which she had again opened for her people." This was the Geneva Bible of 1560. "The Bible," said Chillingworth a conformist, "and the Bible alone is the religion of Protestants."

Another vital principle of the Puritans was the concern to worship God in the beauty of holiness. They sought to purge worship of all Roman accretions, and of every practice not sanctioned by the Word of God. They desired simplicity and reality in worship and so that the worship should be acceptable to God they laid much emphasis on the state of the worshipper's heart, which should be contrite, humble, believing, obedient. Preaching was the most important part of the service, although prayer and Scripture reading prepared for it. The pulpit was placed in a central position in Nonconformist churches and from it the Word of God was expounded thoroughly, in all its parts, week by week. Nothing so roused their anger as unworthy clergy involved in holy things in an unworthy manner. Milton waxed eloquent regarding this in his poem Lycidas, and his pamphlet *The Reason of Church Government Urged against Prelacy* (1641).

Yet again, the strongest influence on the Puritans was their consciousness of the Sovereignty of God in creation, providence and redemption. They sought to live with a keen sense of responsibility to the Almighty, both for themselves, and for others. They felt that they lived in the sight of God and in the presence of eternity. They were in deadly earnest about the value of the soul, the reality of divine judgement, and democratic rights and duties. There is little doubt that there was an atmosphere of moral slackness and decadence at the beginning of the seventeenth century that challenged all that Puritanism stood for. But the authorities of the national Church opposed the men who would have brought about reform, drove them out, and took the part of the licentious court of Charles II. In all the Puritan groups was to be found a strong belief in personal holiness, personal allegiance to God revealed in Christ, as distinct from mere nominal membership of a church on the basis of infant baptism. From this it followed that the Puritan viewed every walk and duty of life as related to his walk with God and obedience to him. This, in turn, gave them the vision of a holy nation governed by godly men. It was this that underlay the efforts of the Puritans when in authority during the Commonwealth, to force others into Puritan patterns of behaviour. This unwise zeal, more than anything else, has given Puritanism a bad name even today.

5

As to Puritanism and the Arts, later generations of writers have caricatured Puritans as gloomy, sour-faced, sanctimonious people, who never laughed and were opposed to all recreation, drama, dancing, music etc. Nothing is further from the truth. They appreciated and enjoyed these where they were wholesome, but strongly attacked them for being debased and corrupting as they often were. The two greatest poets of the age were Spenser and Milton, both Puritans. Cromwell and other leading Puritans delighted in music; much music was published in the Commonwealth period, and the only objection Puritans had was to profane music on the Sabbath. *The Pilgrim's Progress* again and again shows us men and women engaged in singing and dancing, and music at meals in the Interpreter's House. The Puritans developed congregational singing in place of the service being sung by clergy and choir alone. As to the drama, Puritans opposed stage plays in Stuart days because the plays were decidedly bawdy and salacious, especially the Restoration comedies, where the stock themes were murder, adultery, incest and seduction. John Evelyn and Samuel Pepys, who cannot be suspected of Puritan sympathies, expressed their disgust at the profane, atheistical, and licentious plays they saw. As to recreation, the Puritans opposed bear-baiting, cock-fighting, rope-walking and May Day revels, because too often they were associated with drunkenness, gambling, brutality and impurity. The Maypole sounds harmless enough, but in fact it was at the centre of the May Day celebrations a continuation of a pagan festival, rowdy and licentious. The activities associated with May Day had been denounced by the Church long before the Puritan era, for example by the Bishop of Salisbury in the thirteenth century, as encouraging gross immorality. Drunkenness also was widespread and the Puritans endeavoured to check it.

As for Sunday, the Puritans regarded it as a day set apart by God for his service, to be spent, in the words of Richard Baxter, "in hearing the Word of God truly preached, thereby to learn and to do His will; in receiving the sacraments rightly administered; in using public and private prayers; in collecting for the poor and in doing of good works; and chiefly in the true obedience of the inward man". To the Puritan, Sunday was "the market-day of the soul", when they did business especially with God. Sunday sports would interfere with opportunities for religious worship and meditation. King James I in 1618 issued a proclamation scolding the "Puritans and Precisians" and maintaining the right of people to their customary Sunday sports after service, with the exception of bear-baiting and bowling. But so violent were the protests that the king withdrew the order. Charles I aided and abetted by Archbishop Laud re-issued the order in 1633 and issued the *Book of Sports* which outraged the Puritans, and this was one of the issues at Laud's trial. Incidentally, the archbishop was particularly incensed against the Puritans of the Midlands. He reported to the king, "My visitors there found Bedfordshire most tainted (with preaching) of any part of the diocese."

G. M. Trevelyan has an interesting comment on this aspect of Puritanism in his *History of England*: "Family prayer and Bible reading had become national customs among the great majority of religious laymen, whether they were Churchmen or Dissenters. The English character had received an impression from Puritanism which it bore for the next two centuries, though it had rejected Puritan coercion and had driven Dissenters out of polite society. Even the Puritan Sunday survived ... Even at the Restoration when the very name of Puritan was a hissing and a reproach, when the gaols were crowded with harmless Quakers and Baptists, the Puritan idea of Sunday, as a day strictly set aside for rest and religious meditation, continued to hold the allegiance of the English people. The good and evil effects of this self-imposed discipline of a whole nation, in abstaining from organised amusement as well as from work on every seventh day, still awaits the dispassionate study of the social historian." It is interesting also to find that the Restoration Parliament in 1677 copied the Lord's Day legislation of the Commonwealth, confirming existing Acts which laid down that everyone should attend Church, and imposed fines on those who engaged in Sunday travelling or trading, stating that goods exposed to sale were to be confiscated.

As to social affairs, the Puritans stood for bringing Christian principles and Christian concern into the life of the nation. Oliver Cromwell writing to the Speaker of the House of Commons after the astonishing victory of Dunbar, is typical. After describing how God had given them the victory, he proceeds—"We that serve you beg of you not to own us, but God alone ... Disown yourselves; but own your Authority; and improve it to curb the proud and insolent, such as would disturb the tranquility of England, though under what specious pretences soever. Relieve the oppressed, hear the groans of poor prisoners in England. Be pleased to reform the abuses of all professions—and if there be anyone that makes many poor to make a few rich, that suits not a Commonwealth. If He that strengthens your servants to fight, please to give you hearts to set upon these things, in order to His glory and the glory of your Commonwealth—then besides the benefit England shall feel thereby, you shall shine forth to other nations, who shall emulate the glory of such a pattern, and through the power of God turn in to the like! These are our desires. And that you may have liberty and opportunity to do these things, and not be hindered, we have been and shall be (by God's assistance) willing to venture our lives."

Into this confused and troubled nation, where religion and politics, divine right of kings and justification by faith alone, predestination and universal male suffrage, rule by bishops and the priesthood of all believers, reform of abuses and government in a single person, tonnage and poundage and treasure in Heaven, were mixed, came John Bunyan on the threshold of his extraordinary career, which was to make him one of England's greatest writers and a household name.

3

Soldier under Fairfax

1

While John Bunyan was growing up quietly at Elstow great political, social and religious movements and events were causing an increasing stir in the country as a whole. The impact of these matters had effect on Bedfordshire and the little village in which John lived. But he was not so concerned with them at first as with learning his father's skill as a brazier, at the forge attached to the cottage in the fields at Harrowden. This apprenticeship gave him both an intimate knowledge of the craft, and all the necessary skills to earn his own living in due course. It was also affecting his physical development, for he was growing up a tall, broad-shouldered lad, with brawny arms, whose abundant auburn hair added to his striking appearance.

His happy home life was suddenly shattered in the summer of 1644, when there swept over the village, a strange epidemic with which the physicians were quite unable to cope. In those days the rules of health and cleanliness were little understood, or if they were understood, were little regarded. Probably the illness was a form of influenza, but before the end of June his mother Margaret lay in her grave, and John wandered disconsolate about the lanes. A month later his sorrow was further increased when his beloved sister Margaret, fourteen years of age, his playmate as long as he could remember, was buried in the adjoining plot in Elstow churchyard. It was a numbing experience for John but a worse blow was to follow. For within a month his father Thomas married for the third time, in indecent haste to John's mind. If his father and mother are shadowy figures to us, even more so is Thomas's third wife, for we do not even know her name. No doubt Thomas had good reason to secure a wife to look after himself and his home, especially since he was often away working at his trade, but to John it seemed like disloyalty to his mother.

We can imagine John flying for sympathy to his Aunt Rose married to Edward Bunyan, Thomas's brother, who seems to have kept some sort of ale house; and it is not unlikely that they suggested his enlistment in the Parliamentary army, with its convenient opportunity to leave home. It may well have been also that the loss of his mother and sister at an impressionable age, and the quick re-marriage of his father, impelled John to the wild and wilful ways of the next few years, which he lived to describe so vividly and to repent so bitterly. The preaching, also, of Christopher Hall, Vicar of Elstow, a Parliamentarian whose son was baptized "Oliver", may have had something to do with his entering the army.

2

The first Civil War, 1642-46, though having momentous effects on the country as a whole, had not so far in 1644 greatly affected Bedfordshire. Some historians have endeavoured to maintain that the Civil War was a class war, but there were noblemen and gentry, yeomen and peasants on both sides. Dr Maurice Ashley has conclusively repudiated the "class struggle" notion in his valuable book, *The English Civil War*. The complex and intricate causes of the war were both political and religious. There were grievances about arbitrary taxation without consent of Parliament, arguments about property rights, demands for a larger role for

Parliament, and complaints about the organisation and restrictive practices of the Established Church, and about the evil counsellors of the king.

King Charles I came to the throne in 1625 at the age of twenty-five. His father, James I had been a shrewd politician, but Charles was reserved, proud and unyielding, and fully convinced of his "divine right" to govern. He had the misfortune to inherit as his chief minister the Duke of Buckingham, who was arrogant, unscrupulous and unpopular. His unrealistic foreign policy involved England in war with Spain. For this war the king demanded large supplies of money from the House of Commons, which granted a limited subsidy of £140,000, but refused more until various grievances had been remedied. Concern was also felt in many quarters, not only Puritan, because Charles had just married a Roman Catholic French princess. The nation had not forgotten the Spanish Armada and the attempt to conquer England and make her a Catholic country once more.

In Parliament Sir John Eliot, a Cornish squire, took over the leadership of the House, and attempted to impeach Buckingham over the complete failure of the attack on Spain the previous year. The king ordered Eliot's arrest and dissolved the House. Charles declared to Parliament that it was his right alone to summon Parliaments, and that if they opposed his will he would do without them. He then endeavoured to obtain forced loans from landowners but he never had sufficient money for the war. So, when in 1628 he called a Third Parliament, the Commons led by Pym, Eliot and Hampden, once more refused money supplies until grievances such as forced loans, compulsory billeting, arbitrary imprisonment, and the imposition of martial law, had been dealt with. A "Petition of Right" presented to the king in 1628, the year of John Bunyan's birth, setting forth these grievances, was grudgingly accepted.

In 1629 Parliament again criticized illegal taxation (tonnage and poundage), and the growth of Popery and Arminianism. Charles in anger prorogued the Commons, which was not to meet again for eleven years. The king made peace with Spain and France, reduced his revenues, the yield from the Customs rose to £400,000 a year, money was borrowed from the City of London, and so the Government managed to make ends meet. In religion Charles had favoured the Arminians, appointing bishops and higher clergy of that persuasion. He also issued *The Book of Sports* which so angered the Puritans with regard to the misuse of Sunday, approved the wearing of the vestments, and the placing of the Holy Table against the chancel end in the position of an altar. Those who did not comply were brought before the Court of Star Chamber and punished severely.

3

Two other immediate causes of the Civil War were the question of "Ship money", and the Scottish resistance to Church of England Prayer Book usage. Ship money had been levied in past days to provide ships for the defence of British shores, but gathered only from coastal ports. Now, however, Charles decided to levy the tax on all parts of the country, and a storm of protest arose. John Hampden, a great patriot and leader of the Opposition in the House of Commons, refused to pay, and although at his trial in 1638 seven of the twelve judges found for the king, it was plain that the whole nation was in sympathy with his opposition. In Scotland, Charles's attempt to force the Prayer Book system of religion on an unwilling people met with determined opposition. There was a near-riot in St Giles Cathedral, Edinburgh in 1638. Ministers, nobles and gentry, poured into Edinburgh to organize national resistance, and re-stated and signed a National Covenant expressing solidarity to maintain the Scottish Church establishment and way of life against English interference. The Kirk of Scotland had existed since 1567 when Mary, Queen of Scots had abdicated, and it held strongly to its own Calvinist Confession of Faith, its organisation of presbyteries and synods, and to the election of its own ministers.

Events now gathered momentum. Charles set about gathering an army at York with which to confront the Scots and force on them his policies. But shortage of money and lack of enthusiasm amongst his English subjects, paralysed his efforts. Across the border General Leslie and the Earl of Montrose gathered 20,000 men to march on England. In April 1640 Charles was forced to summon what was known as the "Short Parliament", but it declared as before that no money would be forthcoming until security was had for freedom of worship, property, and the liberties of Parliament. After only three weeks the king dissolved Parliament. The Earl of Strafford became Commander-in-chief of the army. But the Scots army of the Covenant under Montrose crossed the Tyne and routed the English cavalry. The king was obliged to accept the Treaty of Ripon by which he agreed to allow the Scottish army to remain in Northumberland and Durham, and to pay its expenses. Charles had now no alternative but to call another Parliament to Westminster. This met on 3rd November, 1640 and its proceedings led directly to the Civil War.

Most of the members were country gentlemen, many related to one another with a fair sprinkling of lawyers and merchants. Nine-tenths of them were critical of the king's counsellors and their proceedings. There was an air of restlessness and uncertainty about them. Charles made an opening speech in which he declared that the Scots were rebels, and that Parliament must provide money to buy them off English soil. Pym summed up the grievances of the nation against the government, and complained of attacks on Parliamentary privileges, illegal taxation, and innovations in religion. Strafford was impeached, sent to the Tower and, in spite of promises of protection by the king, was executed. The Court of Star Chamber and the Court of High Commission were abolished. Laud was sent to the Tower. Ship money was declared illegal. Pym introduced a "Grand Remonstrance" in which all the grievances of the people against the Government were listed as a kind of manifesto to the nation. It was passed at midnight on November 22nd by

159 votes to 148. Oliver Cromwell declared that had it not been passed he and other members would have left England for ever.

The voting—although little more than half the members were present—showed that Parliament was almost equally divided. Angry at the turn events had taken Charles led a small armed party to the House of Commons in order to arrest Pym and four other members, together with Lord Mandeville, the future Earl of Manchester and Parliamentary commander, for treason. The accused members were safely hidden by friends and Charles' plan was thwarted. Civil war now became almost inevitable, and both sides began to organise their supporters and to collect arms and funds. The heart of the question was, "Where did actual sovereign government lie—with the king and his cronies, or with a legally appointed Parliament elected by the nation?" The eventual issue was the liberties of the people and a constitutional monarchy, though this was far in the future. Charles raised his standard at Nottingham on the 22nd August 1640. Parliament appointed the Earl of Essex to command the Parliamentary army, and the Earl of Warwick to take command of the Navy. The Civil War had begun.

4

The Parliamentary party in the Civil War was, very largely, the Puritan party. Richard Baxter is explicit on this: "The generality of people through the land who were then called Puritans, precisioners, religious persons ... adhered to the Parliament. And on the other side the gentry who were not so precise and strict against gaming, or plays, or drinking, nor troubled themselves so much about the matter of God and the world to come. ... And all the sober men that I was acquainted with, who were against the Parliament, were wont to say, 'The king hath the better cause, but the Parliament hath the better men.' "

John Bunyan and his father discussed these matters over the forge as news filtered down to them from London, or was gleaned in public houses, or in the homes of the wealthy where they were not infrequently called to work. Thomas remained a convinced Royalist, and even named a son Charles in May 1645. But Bedfordshire was strongly Parliamentarian in sympathy, though there were some Royalists in the county. With the shires of Northampton, Leicester, Derby, Rutland, Nottingham, Huntingdon and Buckingham, Bedfordshire belonged to the Midland Association of counties supporting the Parliament. A few skirmishes took place in the neighbourhood. Sir Lewis Dyve of Bromham Hall, a leading Bedfordshire royalist, with a small number of men was attacked by troops under Sir Samuel Luke, M.P. for Bedford in July 1642, and escaped only by swimming the Ouse. The next year, when John Hampden had been killed at Chalgrove Field, and John Pym lay dying in London, his life work accomplished, Sir Lewis returned to have his revenge. Coming to Amphill with 400 men he surprised the Bedfordshire Committee appointed by Parliament, and took several of the leading country gentry prisoners to Oxford, headquarters of the King. Pressing on to Bedford he took prisoner Sir John Norwich and other Parliamentary officers, seized 300 horses, and plundered the town and district. Shortly after this Colonel Montague with a small Parliamentary force entered Bedford pretending to be Royalists and took away horses and money intended for the king.

Bunyan would note some of these comings and goings, and see parties of conscripts pressed into the Parliament's forces marching along the roads. In 1643, Sir Samuel Luke, now Governor of the Parliamentary Garrison at Newport Pagnell, Bucks, issued warrants requiring all able-bodied men between sixteen and sixty years of age to report at Leighton Buzzard for military duty and the defence of Parliament and its cause. They had to bring arms and weapons with them. The response was poor, for men were naturally loath to leave their fields at harvest time, and abandon their jobs and families for uncertain and dangerous tasks, however much they believed in the cause. In the autumn of 1644 Sir Samuel's recruiting officers came to Elstow to gather Bedfordshire's proportion of men required for the defence of the Newport garrison. John Bunyan, hearing of this, took his chance to leave home.

5

He was a tall, vigorous youth, and although under age—being only fifteen-and-a-half years old—he looked older than he was. He was adept at lying, as he says himself, and it was easy to convince the recruiting officers that he was sixteen. Newport Pagnell was a strategic point on the road between London and Yorkshire, which had been captured by the Earl of Essex and was now a strongly fortified garrison town. It was twelve miles from Bedford to Newport Pagnell and the company of impressed men marching along the Roman Akerman Street did not find it hard going. What John's thoughts were we cannot say, but probably he was much relieved to have left home and excited at the unknown possibilities before him. Sir Samuel Luke was appointed Governor, and the fortress remained in Parliamentary hands for the remainder of the war. So, as a mere lad, although certainly "able-bodied", John Bunyan found himself a soldier (or centinel) in the New Model Army commanded by Sir Thomas Fairfax, "Black Tom" as his troops loved to call him.

Early biographers of Bunyan were concerned with the possibility that John served in the Royalist ranks in the Civil War. J. A. Froude gave it as his opinion that Bunyan was a Royalist because his father was, and because John Gifford, later Minister at Bedford, had been a Royalist major. The reasoning is absurd. John Bunyan was not in sympathy with his father at the time he entered the army; Bedfordshire was a Parliamentary county on whom levies of conscripts were made; while John did not meet Gifford until years after the Civil War. Had Bunyan been on the Royalists' side it is certain that his imprisonment would have been vastly different if not avoided altogether.

But the side on which Bunyan fought has been put beyond

all doubt by the discovery at the Record Office of the Muster Rolls of the Newport Garrison from 1644 to 1647. On November 30, 1644 John Bunyan was a private or as it was then termed a "centinel" in the company commanded by Colonel Richard Cockayne. On March 22nd 1645 he appears in the list of Major Boulton's company and he was regularly mustered in the major's company up to May 27th 1645. His presence at Newport Pagnell on May 27th 1645 renders impossible the theory that he was present at the siege of Leicester. And Bunyan was still a member of one of the companies making up the force at the Newport garrison as late as June 17th 1647. Colonel Richard Cockayne under whom Bunyan served was a Bedfordshire man of some note, who may well have known the Bunyan family. John Bunyan served in the Parliamentary ranks, not for a few months as so many writers have affirmed, but for about three years. This is a considerable period in the most impressionable part of a young man's life.

The officers under whom John and his fellow recruits served were often bearded, relatively well-dressed, with high-plumed hats, armoured breast-plates, knee breeches, and high leather boots. When the New Model Army was complete in 1645, Cromwell's officers were supplied with red coats, and uniforms became part of the common soldier's equipment. John's own uniform consisted of a plain brown doublet and coat or "cassock", short breeches, two shirts, stockings of "good Welsh cotton", and shoes tied with laces. He also wore a Monmouth cap, knitted, blocked, and tasselled. His weapon was a short musket—presuming that he was a musketeer, though it is possible that he was a pikeman. The bullets were quite heavy and with twelve charges of powder, were fastened in a leather bandolier worn over his shoulder and fitted with small pouches. The infantryman was paid at the rate of eightpence a day, the cavalry trooper three times as much. If John was a pikeman he would have worn helmet, breast- and back plates, and metal thigh guards. The pike was sixteen feet in length, but it was quite common for the soldiers to reduce the length to make it less unwieldy. The pikemen were chosen from the strongest and tallest men in the unit, and it is on account of this that some suppose John to have been a pikeman. At the same time, at fifteen and a half years he was not likely to be very tall.

At Newport Pagnell, Sir Samuel Luke the Governor, an ardent Presbyterian, a valiant energetic officer and a man of sense and courage, lived in a house on the Green, but used as his military headquarters the "Saracen's Head". John was probably billeted in a house, or he may have lived in a tent, at least in the summer. If billeted with a family he would doubtless have made friends there, and this may account for certain circumstances to be discussed later. Much of his time would be occupied with drill. The musket (if Bunyan was a musketeer and not a pikeman and there were two musketeers to every pikeman) was cumbersome, and if not carefully handled was almost as dangerous to the owner as to the enemy. It had an over-all length of about five feet, and firing a 1¼ ounce bullet was effective at a hundred yards. Because of the length and weight of the musket it required a rest which was spiked at one end for fixing in the ground, and forked at the other end to take the musket's weight. The battle formation for the foot soldiers was usually six or four deep, each rank firing and then falling back to the rear to re-load. Pike drill was basically more simple than musket drill, and depended for its effectiveness on numbers, to produce the "hedgehog" front to charging horse, and to provide a tightly knit mass of pike and armour for "push of pike." A small sword called a hanger was also carried by the foot soldiers.

6

Discipline in the New Model Army was strict and well supervised. To Oliver Cromwell it was a new kind of recruitment—"to raise such men as had the fear of God before them, and made some conscience of what they did". With so many religious men in its ranks, Presbyterians, Independents and others, the officers and leaders of the regiments and companies were chosen for their moral character and principles as well as for their fighting abilities. The officers were concerned with the moral and religious lives of their men, as well as with their effectiveness in battle. In May 1643 Oliver wrote of his men, "No man swears but he pays his twelve-pence: if he is in drink he is set in the sticks, or worse; if one calls the other 'Roundhead' he is cashiered; in so much that the countries where they come leap for joy of them." Offences against persons and property were severely punished. The actual military discipline was also severe. In April 1643 Cromwell had two troopers who had deserted whipped in the market place of Huntingdon, and then "turned off" as renegades. One wonders how often John Bunyan was fined for swearing!

Vera Brittain whose book, *In the Steps of John Bunyan* is both a comprehensive and percipient account of John, thinks that too many biographers "present a lusty young tinker and reprobate as the incarnation of moral purity". She points out that although in *Grace Abounding* paragraph 315, he definitely asserted that he was not guilty of adultery and fornication, yet in paragraphs 8 and 9 he clearly states his acquaintance with carnal sin. "Until I came to the state of marriage," he says, "I was the very ringleader of all the youth that kept me company, in all manner of vice and ungodliness." She suggests also that there were brothels in Newport Pagnell. This is extremely unlikely, as such would not have been tolerated by the Parliamentary authorities, though they were all too common where the Royalists were in power. In a later chapter we shall examine Bunyan's opinion of himself in his famous autobiography. But the severe discipline in the Parliamentary army would argue against his early indulgence in the lusts of the flesh. Godly officers superintended the habits of those under their command. Further, at Newport Pagnell there was constant preaching in the parish church by Independent and other preachers, and Bunyan would soon become acquainted with the main points of Puritan theology, which laid great emphasis on holiness. Serious discussions and debates were often held between those of differing views, on the doctrines of Scripture, and the best form of church government and the conduct of the State. One can imagine John Bunyan taking a curious interest in them. That these spiritual exercises did not convert him may surprise us, but until God made John's heart ready to receive him, he was indifferent to spiritual things.

The Parliamentary authorities made an effort to provide for the spiritual welfare of their soldiers. There were chaplains to regiments. In October 1644 Sir Samuel Luke mentioned that there were no fewer than seven "able divines" in the garrison at Newport Pagnell. Two sermons were preached to the troops every Sabbath and one every Thursday, while prayers, with the reading of a chapter from the Bible, were held every morning before the placing of the guards. No soldier was allowed out of his billet after nine o'clock at night. A strongly religious atmosphere permeated the Parliamentary ranks. Fast days and Days of Humiliation were kept at intervals. Whenever possible battles were preceded by some form of religious services. After Naseby and Marston Moor the victorious Parliamentary forces sang a psalm of thanksgiving and held a solemn celebration the following Sunday. There were between seven and eight thousand men in the garrison at Newport, many, like Bunyan, young conscripts. Inevitably they unconsciously absorbed democratic opinions and the religious fervour of the army chaplains and the preaching colonels.

Each Parliamentary soldier was issued with a copy of *The Souldiers Pocket Bible* consisting of extracts from the Geneva Bible. It had the "imprimatur" of Edmund Calamy, an eminent Puritan, and was arranged under such headings as "A Souldier must not doe wickedly", "A Souldier must be valiant for God's Cause", "A Souldier must love his enemies as they are his enemies, and hate them as they are God's enemies." "A Souldier must crie unto God in his heart in the very instant of battell." The Pocket Bible, it was stated "may bee also usefull for any Christian to meditate upon, now in this miserable time of Warre."

John would also have a copy of *The Souldiers Catechisme* composed for the Parliamentary army by Robert Ram,

Minister of Spalding. It was "Written for the encouragement and instruction of all that have taken up Armes in this Cause of God and His people; especially the common Souldiers". It answered in a fashion satisfactory to the Parliamentary side such questions as, "Is it not against the King that you fight in this cause?" The answer is, "No surely. Wee take up armes against the enemies of Jesus Christ, who in His Majesties name make warre against the Church and People of God." Parliamentary propaganda was certainly not neglected.

Oliver Cromwell's second son Captain Oliver Cromwell, aged 21, was in the garrison force at Newport Pagnell, but John Bunyan missed contact with him for in March 1644 Oliver's son died of smallpox at Newport. He was described in a newspaper of the time as "a civil young gentleman and the joy of his father". It is not known where he is buried or whether his father attended the funeral. But when Bunyan arrived there in the autumn he was to see the great Parliamentary commander and later Lord Protector, Oliver himself. For Oliver was at Newport Pagnell sometime before the battle of Naseby and inspected the troops and garrison defences. Standing among them as they were drawn up in rank John Bunyan saw Oliver and his staff officers, and must have been impressed by the Protector's determined look and noble bearing. It is not impossible that John was one of those appointed to mount guard over Oliver's quarters while he was in the town.

As to what active military service he saw in the field we know little. Small companies of soldiers, chosen by lot, were sometimes sent by the Governor on marauding expeditions to seize horses or food, or to besiege castles and manors belonging to Royalists in the neighbourhood. On one occasion John had an escape he recorded in *Grace Abounding* twenty years later. "When I was a soldier, I with others, were drawn out to go to such a place to beseige it; but when I was just ready to go, one of the company desired to go in my room; to which, when I had consented, he took my place; and coming to the siege, as he stood sentinel, he was shot into the head with a musket bullet, and he died."

The use of the word "siege" in this passage, has persuaded some biographers to suppose that Bunyan was present at the siege of Leicester. But Charles I began the investment of that town on May 28th, 1645, and we know that John was at Newport Pagnell on May 27th. He could not therefore have been at Leicester. The reference in his autobiography must refer to the siege of a fortified house somewhere in the vicinity of the garrison town. It is most tantalising that this is the only reference to active service during the whole three years he was in the army. A friend of the writer served during the Second World War in the Burma campaign, ending with the rank of Colonel. He went through the whole campaign with all its horrors, disasters, and sufferings. When he left the army he was converted, and became active in Christian work just as Bunyan was to do. But of all he saw and experienced in Burma he could not be persuaded to say one single word. Perhaps the suffering and horrors were too deeply etched on his memory, or he had been forced to do things which he later saw were inconsistent with his Christian profession. Surely this was the exact condition of John Bunyan. Looking back on his army career, hearing the cries and noise of battle and siege, remembering his share in it, insignificant though it may have been, remembering comrades who had been killed or wounded—he kept it all locked up in his memory, and wrote barely a sentence of it all. This, in part, may well have contributed to his tumult of conscience in later days.

References are made in *The Holy War* (1682), to marches, war plans, sieges, and parleys, but all too vague to connect with any soldiering Bunyan may have done. All we can be certain of is that he acquired some general military knowledge. One possibility is likely, however, and that is that Bunyan was present at the battle of Naseby on June 14th 1645, when the Parliamentary army under Fairfax and Cromwell overwhelmed and destroyed the Royalists. It was a decisive victory since it put an end to Charles' main field force. It is known that several regiments from Newport Pagnell were at Naseby under Fairfax, and it is not improbable that Bunyan was among them. But he gives us no word!

7

At Newport Pagnell John Bunyan became acquainted with three persons who, in years to come, he was to know well for they became his life-long friends. We shall consider their relationship to him in due course, but here we will just note their names and occupations.

The Rev John Gibbs was appointed Vicar of Newport Pagnell in 1646, replacing an adherent to the old ecclesiastical regime. He was the son of a cooper at Bedford and a student of Sidney Sussex College, Cambridge, a Puritan foundation where Cromwell had been a student. In days to come he was to give Bunyan considerable help and to be helped by him.

At Newport Pagnell also, lived Matthias Cowley, who seems to have kept a stationer's or bookseller's shop, and whom Bunyan got to know extremely well. It has been suggested that it was in his shop that John first read Milton's *Paradise Lost*. As a soldier, Bunyan had no idea that one day he would become a celebrated author, and neither did Cowley, yet in days to come he would publish several of John's writings.

Then there was William Dell, one of the Puritan chaplains to the garrison. He had trained for the ministry at Emmanuel College, Cambridge, foster-mother of so many Puritan divines. He was a famous preacher: when he preached in an orchard before Sir Samuel Luke's tent, hundreds of soldiers crowded to hear him, some even climbing the trees to do so. "There hath been," he declared, "a very sensible presence of God with us; we have seen His goings, and observed His very footsteps, for He hath dwelt among us, and marched at the head of us, step by step." Dell was high in favour with the Parliamentary leaders, and in June 1646 officiated at the wedding of Cromwell's daughter Bridget to General Ireton. John's friendship with this remarkable man lay many years ahead, but they were destined to be associated in Gospel preaching in close and harmonious fellowship.

So we have but glimpses of John, soldiering at Newport, growing up robust, strong-willed, excitable, noting with his keen brain all the practical side of military practice and manoeuvres and storing up details that he was to use in *The Holy War*.

8

On June 26th, 1645, after the battle of Naseby, Sir Samuel Luke's governorship of the garrison ended, owing to the passing by the Commons of the "Self-denying Ordinance" by which members of Parliament undertook to resign all military commands. He continued to represent Bedford for some years, but retired before the Restoration and died in 1670. John Bunyan and his fellow soldiers found themselves under a new Governor, Captain Charles D'Oyley, recommended by Sir Thomas Fairfax. Soon afterwards the garrison was reduced to 800 foot and 120 horse. During the autumn and winter of 1645-46 the soldiers had little to do, though regular drill and preaching went on. Two rivers meet at Newport Pagnell, the Ouse and the Lovat, and no doubt John who was a keen angler, joined with other men to fish the waters.

Then, on August 6th 1646, surprising news reached Newport Pagnell. Because of the decline of the king's cause, several garrisons were to be abandoned, and the soldiers employed for service in Ireland for "the relief of Protestants." The garrisons of Cambridge, Huntingdon, Bedford, and Newport Pagnell were thereupon relinquished, and the "Committee for Irish Affairs" of both Houses of Parliament ordered the army at Newport Pagnell to be sent to Chester. John Bunyan, by now happily adjusted to military life, was in no great hurry to return to Elstow, to his royalist father and unknown step-mother. So he volunteered for Ireland, and was put into Colonel Robert Hammond's regiment, his company commander being Captain Charles O'Hara. Robert Hammond was a kinsman of Oliver Cromwell, soon to be appointed Governor of Carisbrooke Castle on the Isle of Wight, where Charles I was to be confined at the pleasure of Parliament in 1647.

John, however, was not to see the emerald isle. Hammond's regiment, including John, duly marched to Chester in March 1647, in advance of the main body. Here John saw mountains high and foreboding such as he had never seen in the flat countryside of Bedfordshire. At Chester the regiment was recalled to army headquarters at Saffron Walden, and was soon to be moved to St Albans. At Saffron Walden the majority of soldiers refused to serve in Ireland, their objections being put to the army command by democratic representatives from each regiment. But a minority of six officers and 400 men were willing to go to Ireland. Among these was centinel John Bunyan, who under Captain O'Hara, along with the others was marched back to Newport Pagnell to await fresh orders. Thus John's name appears on the Muster Roll of O'Hara's company on 17th June 1647. The journey to Ireland was eventually cancelled and John's regiment was disbanded late in July 1647. He had thus been almost three years a soldier in the Parliamentary army, had seen and learned much, and was now a tinker again. He reached the cottage at Harrowden soon after Bedford and district had become the headquarters of Fairfax's forces. Some 20,000 men were encamped in the surrounding area, while Fairfax, Cromwell and Ireton were in constant discussion over negotiations with the king, which unfortunately came to nothing. The king was a prisoner and militant Puritanism was in power. But John thought little of these matters. He was a civilian again, about to take up work on his own, and even more momentous for him—to get married.

4

Troubled Tinker

1

Life as a soldier had been singularly care-free. Taking up civilian life again brought many trials, anxieties, and conflicts of conscience. He had left home a boy; he returned a man. We do not know how he was received at the cottage in the fields, but very probably he was warmly welcomed, especially as Thomas now had an additional helper at the forge and on his daily rounds. Thomas had written to his son at Newport Pagnell several times, giving him the local news, such as the visit of Oliver Cromwell with 600 horse to Bedford in June 1645, and how in August the king himself with 300 Royalist horse had plundered the village of Goldington, and how Charles had entered Bedford only to be driven off by Lt-Col Richard Cokayn, who fought a brilliant rear-guard action at Bedford Bridge. Family news had been sent too, such as the death of John's half-brother Charles in May 1645, and the birth of another brother, Thomas, a year later.

Events in the nation seemed to go from bad to worse. The Parliamentary party was almost fiercely divided, the Presbyterians in league with the Scots, demanding uniformity of worship on the Geneva model, and the Independents, especially those in the army (where they were in a majority), seeking toleration and freedom of conscience, and the setting up of Independent Churches on Congregational lines. Both sections were endeavouring to come to terms with Charles, who played off one against the other. It was a sad day for England when the Commons lost Hampden and Pym, wise and constructive statesmen who might well have resolved matters with a constitutional monarchy. If this had been brought about, and it is not certain that it could have been for Charles was a most tricky and unreliable monarch, the Puritans would have been spared persecution, and John Bunyan his twelve years' imprisonment.

He did not spend over-much time puzzling over national events. To begin with he flung himself into his father's work; the old skill soon returned, and soon also his seven-year apprenticeship to his father was completed, and he himself recognized and accepted as a fully trained brazier, under the Statute of Apprentices. His step-mother and her children doubtless made the cottage a happy home, but increasingly John felt that he did not belong to it and constantly thought of seeking a home of his own. He was nineteen years of age.

To set himself up as an independent tinker or brazier Bunyan had to make or acquire the tools required for his trade. No doubt with the approval and help of his father John acquired a hammer, soldering iron, a pair of pliers, snippers for cutting tin, and a "roundhead" for shaping the lids of kettles and saucepans. Most important and more costly, was an anvil, and John decided that he would forge this heavy instrument himself, with the help of a Bedford moulder whom he knew. It had a spear-point to hold it firm in a metal or wooden base and when it was finished it weighed sixty pounds. When it was completed he carved his name on it—J. BVNYAN, and on the other side the date 1647 and the word "HELSTOWE". In 1905 this very anvil was discovered in a marine store in St. Neots where it had lain for forty years. Its history was carefully traced back through a number of owners, and ultimately, it is alleged, to an Elstow innkeeper who took the anvil and some other tools from John Bunyan to pay a debt. There is some doubt about the latter part of this story, but that the anvil was actually John Bunyan's there is no doubt. The signature has been compared to other Bunyan signatures known to be genuine, and the V in BVNYAN agrees with the same letter in John's copy of Foxe's *Book of Martyrs*. Other experts have examined the anvil and declare it to be of seventeenth century workmanship. It is now one of the most prized Bunyan relics at the Bunyan Meeting in Mill Street, Bedford.

2

The shock of horror that swept through England at the trial and execution of Charles I on January 30, 1649 reached Elstow also, but we have no means of knowing how John reacted to it. He was busy with his work, perhaps preparing for marriage, or even enjoying married life. For he married in 1648 or 1649. We have no knowledge of the date, or the church where he was married, or even the name of his first wife. All he tells us in *Grace Abounding*, paragraph 15, is—"Presently after this, I changed my condition into a married state, and my mercy was to light upon a wife whose father was counted godly. This woman and I, though we came together as poor as poor might be (not having so much household stuff as a dish or spoon betwixt us both) ..."

There is no registration of this marriage in any of the parish registers of Elstow, Bedford or neighbouring places. Because of the Civil War registers were not scrupulously kept and were sometimes destroyed. When in 1645 Parliament dissolved the Established Church as it had previously existed, marriages were allowed to be made before a magistrate, whose records also were often carelessly kept, lost or destroyed. Bunyan's wife may have been a childhood friend from Elstow, or someone he had met at Bedford. But it is equally possible, and much more likely, that John met her at Newport Pagnell when he was a soldier. She may well have been a relation or friend of John's bookseller friend Matthias Cowley. She may have been a member of the family with which John was billeted. We do not even know her name, but from the fact that often in those days the first-born daughter was called after her mother, and John's elder daughter was called Mary, his first wife might well have been Mary. Of her surname we have no knowledge. She would appear to have been an orphan. Strange as it may seem, she was never a member of the Bedford Puritan Church, but appears to have remained an Anglican.

John and Mary Bunyan (if Mary was indeed her name) rented a small cottage in the main street of Elstow village. It had a lean-to shack at one side which he used as a workshop, and a small garden behind where they probably kept a few chickens. It was cheaply built of timber and pebble stones, and here John found a home brightened by peace and love. Somehow they managed to get some furniture and household things together, from the gifts of friends, well-wishers among his customers, and his own earnings. The cottage pointed out to visitors to Elstow as the one in which John lived is certainly not in the same condition as it was in Bunyan's day, for it has plainly been rebuilt, has a tiled roof whereas Bunyan's cottage was thatched, and the lean-to forge has gone. But it is probably not the original Bunyan cottage at all, for James Copner, Vicar of Elstow for many years, and a local antiquarian, says that Bunyan's cottage was demolished about 1836 and another built on its site.

"There was no imprudence in this early marriage," comments Robert Southey, not because John had a trade to support them, but because "the girl had been trained up in the way she should go." She certainly had, and Bunyan himself describes this as "a mercy". She was gentle, affectionate, and religious. Her father was an Anglican Puritan. "She would be often telling me," says Bunyan in *Grace Abounding*, "what a godly man her father was, and how he would reprove and correct vice, both in his house, and amongst his neighbours; what a strict and holy life he lived in his day both in word and deed." His wife's reminiscences had some spiritual effect on John and made him a more regular church-goer.

3

Mary's dowry consisted of two devotional books left her by her father. The first was, *The Plain Man's Pathway to Heaven*, published in 1601 by Arthur Dent, the parish minister of Shoebury in Essex. It was really a sermon on repentance, and had reached its twenty-fourth edition by 1637. In an Introduction, Puritan Dent assured his readers that his book did not meddle with Church controversies, but only entered on "a controversie with Sathan and sin." It was a book of 423 pages and was in the form of a conversation between Theologus a divine; Philagathas, an honest man; Asunetas, an ignorant man; and Antilegon, a caviller. Such topics as original sin, worldly corruption, salvation and damnation were discussed with light and heat. It made some impression upon John when he first read it, and thirty years later when he was writing *The Life and Death of Mr Badman*, he used the dialogue technique of Arthur Dent.

The second book that Mary Bunyan possessed was *The Practice of Piety*, also very popular in its day especially amongst Puritans. It was published in 1612 by Lewis Bayly of Evesham, afterwards Bishop of Bangor. It was written for the purpose of "directing a Christian how to walke, that hee may please God." James Frazer of Brea, the Minister of Culross and a notable Scottish Presbyterian leader, was converted through reading it. The book consisted of Meditations on "the Essence and Attributes of God, out of the Holy Scriptures".

These two books John and his Mary read together in the evening after the toil of the day was done and he says that "though they did not reach my heart to awaken it about my sad and sinful state, yet they did beget within me some desires after religion; so that, because I knew no better, I fell in very eagerly with the religion of the times; to wit, to go to Church twice a day ... and there should very devoutly both say and sing as others did, yet retaining my wicked life."

The vicar of Elstow was Christopher Hall who was appointed in 1639 by Archbishop Laud, but managed to hold his appointment through the Civil Wars, the Commonwealth and the Protectorate, thanks in part to Cromwell's flexible ecclesiastical policy. The truth was that, although hardly a strict Puritan, he held some of their views in a moderate way, was a supporter of the Parliamentary side in the war, and yet seems to have continued to use the proscribed Prayer Book, or parts of it, at his services. When the Restoration came in 1660 he was allowed to continue in his post. It is difficult to judge whether he was a man of courageous principle, or a Mr Facing-both-ways, but on the whole he would appear to have been the former. To this good man and his services and sermons John Bunyan began constantly to resort, sitting beside Mary on the unvarnished bench near the high oak-carved pulpit, still to be seen in Elstow Church.

Bunyan tells us that in his attendance at the Parish Church he was "so overrun with the spirit of superstition, that I adored, and that with great devotion, even all things (both the High Place, Priest, Clerk, Vestment, Service, and what else) belonging to the Church; counting all things holy that were therein contained, and especially the Priest and Clerk most happy, and without doubt, greatly blessed." It is surprising to see the liturgical service and vestments continued, when Parliament had supposedly suppressed them, and when anything savouring of episcopacy would have secured the ejection of the vicar. But Christopher Hall was attached to the liturgy, and did not abandon the vestments. He was allowed to continue the use of these no doubt because he was a supporter of the Parliament, and also because Elstow was but a small and obscure place.

4

As to what John means by "retaining my wicked life" it is not easy to come to a perfectly satisfying conclusion. It appears that he was a leader of the youth in Elstow, and may even have been a popular hero because of his army experience. No doubt he embroidered many tales of adventures and horrors to eager listeners. "It was my delight," he records, "to be taken captive by the Devil *at his will*, being filled with all unrighteousness ... that from a child I had but few equals both for cursing, swearing, lying, and blaspheming the holy Name of God." Again, "I did still let loose the reins to my lust, and delighted in all transgression against the Law of God: so that, until I came to the state of marriage, I was the very ringleader of all the youth that kept me company, in all manner of vice and ungodliness. Yes, such prevalency had the lusts and fruits of the flesh in this poor soul of mine, that had not a miracle of precious grace prevented, I had not only perished by the stroke of Eternal Justice, but had also laid myself open even to the stroke of those laws which bring some to disgrace and open shame before the face of the world."

He tells us also of his prowess in bell-ringing and various sports. One day, he says, as he was standing at a neighbour's shop-window, "cursing and swearing, and playing the madman after my wonted manner", the woman of the house who was a very loose and ungodly wretch, came out and reproved him, and told him that he was likely to spoil all the youth of the town. This shamed him, and made him wish that his father had not given him such a bad example in this way. Strangely enough, he immediately left off swearing and could "speak better and with more pleasantness than ever I could before". His vocabulary was enlarged and purified.

Probably it is best not to imagine that Bunyan's early years of manhood were spent in extreme profligacy. It must be remembered that the Puritans were great soul-searchers and delighted to "keep close accounts with God", their consciences accusing them severely for the least departure from the strait and narrow way. In October 1638 Oliver Cromwell wrote to his cousin Mrs Oliver St John: "The Lord accept me in His Son, and give me to walk in the light, as He is the light! He it is that enlighteneth our blackness, our darkness. I dare not say He hideth His face from me. He giveth me to see light in His light ... blessed be His name for shining upon so dark a heart as mine! You know what my manner of life hath been. Oh, I lived in, and loved darkness, and hated light; I was a chief, the chief of sinners. This is true: I hated godliness, yet God had mercy on me!" This is a typical Puritan statement of a man who regarded his sins as more heinous than others would. It may equally have been so with John Bunyan whose worst faults were no doubt swearing, lying, drinking, gambling and Sunday sports. And of course these would appear in darker colours after his conversion.

Although Christopher Hall had been appointed to his parish by Laud he did not follow that unfortunate cleric's "Book of Sports", so hated by the Puritans. Indeed, one Sunday the vicar preached a powerful sermon against Sunday sports, no doubt going into details about them and the vile influence they would have on the spiritual life. To John, a great lover of the parson's sermons, this was a blow indeed. He went home conscience-stricken, thinking that Hall had preached the sermon "on purpose to show me my evil-doing". And perhaps he had!

But after a good dinner he shook the sermon out of his mind, and joined his sporting companions on the village green for a game of "Cat". This game is still played in Bedfordshire. On this particular Sunday afternoon John had struck the peg out of the hole into the air, and club in hand he strode after it to strike it again. But before he did so he hesitated, and listened like one who heard an unexpected call. Eternity seemed to take the place of time. "A voice", he tells us, "did suddenly dart from Heaven into my soul, which said, 'Wilt thou leave thy sins and go to Heaven, or have thy sins and go to Hell?' " This is the relevant and immediate question—even for people today! The ultimate alternatives presented themselves to Bunyan there on the village green. He dropped his club to the ground, looked up to Heaven, and it seemed to him as though the Lord Jesus looked down upon him—"hotly displeased with me" on account of his ungodly practices. As he mused he came to the conclusion "that I had been a great and grievous sinner, and that it was now too late for me to look after Heaven; for Christ would not forgive me, nor pardon my transgressions ... I resolved in my mind I would go on in sin: for, thought I, if the case be thus, my state is surely miserable. Miserable if I leave my sins, and but miserable if I follow them." All this and more crossed his mind in an instant between one blow at the "cat" and the next. Although his companions looked at him curiously, he chose to tell them nothing, and they all resumed the game.

5

But the voice from Heaven had deeply impressed him, and the tremendous question with which he was faced—"Heaven or Hell?"—refused to be banished from his mind. Undoubtedly remembered scraps of Puritan sermons heard at Newport Pagnell stirred his conscience. It is most likely that great stress was laid on divine judgement and doom against sin and sinners. What Bunyan needed was a wise and loving person who could show him God's great love and power in sending his Son to take away sin by his sacrifice on the Cross, and that by repentance towards God and faith in the Lord Jesus Christ he could be forgiven, freed from sin, and receive the gift of eternal life. But it seems that no one ever helped John in the spiritual burden of his soul, and for three or four years he was tormented by guilt, doubt, fears and many imagined horrors. The time was to come when the burden would be lifted by the very One he thought looked in condemnation upon him; and it is certain that when he became a true believer and a preacher of the everlasting Gospel he had winsome power, borne of experience, to lead troubled souls to Christ and his grace.

Meanwhile, with Mary, he began to read the Bible, especially the historical parts, but "as for Paul's epistles and suchlike Scriptures, I could not away with them, being as yet but ignorant, either of the corruptions of my nature, or of the want and worth of Jesus Christ to save me." There was some outward reformation in his conduct, which impressed his neighbours who took him "to be a very godly man, a new and religious man, and did marvel much to see such a great and famous alteration in my life and manners.'' But all was not well within. In addition, another burden was added to them. Their first child, a daughter, was born to Mary and John, and on 20th July 1650 Christopher Hall christened her "Mary". They rejoiced in her birth, but to their dismay soon found that she was blind. It was a sore blow to them, particularly to John who later wrote of her—"my poor blind child, who lay nearer my heart than all I had beside''.

Before the divine question came to him on the village green John had greatly enjoyed ringing the bells of Elstow steeple. There are five bells, and tradition has it that Bunyan was in charge of number four. Sunday by Sunday, and at bell-ringing practices, sturdy and muscular John pulled away with all his heart. But now he began to have qualms about it. It was a vanity, not fitting to a religious man. With much regret he gave it up, although so fond of it was he that he would stand in the belfry doorway to watch the ringers. Then the thought came to him. Suppose one of the bells fell on him and killed him! About that very time a flash of lightning had struck a nearby village church and killed a man who was tolling the bell. Or suppose the steeple should fall! John knew that he was not ready to face death as yet, and so the bell-ringing was given up and he kept away from the belfry. But he did not lose the love of the bells, and years later when writing *The Pilgrim's Progress* he made all the bells of the Celestial City ring out to welcome Christian and Hopeful. He even wrote some verses about them:

Bells have wide mouths and tongues, but are too weak,
Have they not help, to sing, or talk, or speak,
But if you move them they will mak't appear
By speaking they'll make all the Town to hear.
When ringers handle them with Art and Skill,
They then the ears of their Observers fill,
With such brave Notes, they ting and tang so well
As to outstrip all with their ding, dong, Bell.

And he ends with this reference to himself and his long-past days:

> O Lord! If Thy poor Child might have his will
> And might his meaning freely to Thee tell,
> He never of this Musick has his fill,
> There's nothing to him like thy ding, dong, Bell.

It was harder still for John to give up dancing, of which he was very fond and he hung on to this pastime for a year, but in the end his accusing conscience bade him give it up also.

All this time Bunyan was very busily engaged in his calling, at his forge adjoining his cottage, or travelling to other villages and to Bedford in pursuit of work. Often the tinker's cry was heard from his lips in village street or Bedford market-place—"Pots to mend, knives to grind", varied with, "Have you any work for a tinker? Have you any old bellows to mend?" Work there was in plenty and he prospered. During 1650 his occupation took him to the village of Willington, four miles east of Bedford. Here was the mansion of the Gostwick family, renowned in English history, one of their ancestors being most valiant at the Field of the Cloth of Gold; another, Sir John Gostwick, Master of the Horse to King Henry the Eighth, helped Thomas Cromwell to suppress the monasteries. Within the Gostwick estate stood two finely built outbuildings, a dove-cote and a cow-house, and John's task was to repair the metal-work on these centuries old structures. The dove-cote, for some reason or other, was called "King Henry's Stable", and here in a large upper chamber stood an open fire-place. On this John carved his name with his tinker's tools:

IOHN BVN
YAN
1650

It is still a fascinating sight for Bunyan lovers.

His inward struggles continued and increased. He saw himself as "nothing but a poor painted hypocrite". But he was proud of his new godliness and did all he could to be seen and be well spoken of by men. No doubt it was also good for business! He made every effort to keep the commandments, and thought that God must be pleased with him. But he was to know later that in God's sight justification by works or human effort was impossible. He was to learn that justification comes only by faith in the sin-atoning work of the Redeemer. This was the great discovery of the Reformation, and Martin Luther's "article of a standing or falling Church." To this experience of trust in the saving mercy of Christ John Bunyan was now to be introduced.

5

Sinner Saved

1

One morning John Bunyan was trundling his barrow through the streets of Bedford intent on getting work from the housewives. His clear voice rang out through the district and many pots, kettles, and scissors were brought to him. In one of the streets he paused between jobs to rest, and as he did so he saw three or four poor women sitting at a door in the sunshine engaged in earnest conversation. That it was not empty gossip John was sure, for there was no laughter to be heard, and every face had a solemn expression as though what they talked about was deadly serious. Curious, he drew near and lingered nearby to hear what it was all about. He soon learned. They were talking about the things of God.

Although he did not yet know it they were among the twelve foundation members of the Puritan Free Church recently established in Bedford, under John Gifford, the first pastor. Bunyan fancied himself as a brisk talker in religion, as Talkative his later invention was, and thought he might as well join in and add his wisdom to theirs. But to his dismay he found himself quite out of his depth; indeed, their conversation was far above and beyond him. "Their talk," he tells us, "was about a new birth, the work of God on their hearts, also how they were convinced of their miserable state by nature. They talked how God had visited their souls with His love in the Lord Jesus, and with what words and promises they had been refreshed, comforted, and supported against the temptations of the devil." Not only the matter of their talk impressed John, though as yet he did not understand it, but also the manner of it, for "they spake as if joy did make them speak; they spake with such pleasantness of Scripture language, and with such appearance of grace in all they said, that they were to me as if they had found a new world." So, indeed, they had, the world of truth and salvation and Christ, instead of that of ignorance and sin and Satan. This was rather like an informal "experience meeting" before the time of John Wesley. How few today get together to tell of God's dealings with their souls, and of his gracious work of sanctification in their lives. Plenty of talk at sunlit doors concerning sport, politics, strikes, inflation, last night's television programme—but how little about the things of God and of eternity!

In one of his illuminating lectures on *Grace Abounding*, Dr Alexander Whyte has this to say about these poor women of Bedford sitting talking in the sunshine. "From this page of John Bunyan we learn this also, what and where is the true Church of Christ on the earth. The true test of a true Church as of a true tree is its fruit. Those three or four poor women were the true tests and the true seals of the true Church of Christ in Bedford. It is of next to no consequence how the Church of Christ is governed, whether by popes, or by cardinals, or by bishops, by presbyters, or by managers: a true Church is known not by its form of government but by its fruits; by the walk and the conversation of its members ... The one thing of any real consequence for a Church is this: What do her people, and especially what do her poor women talk about when they meet and sit down in the sun? 'Have you forgot the close, and the milk-house, and the stable, and the barn, where God did visit your souls?' asks Bunyan of his first readers. That is the true communion roll which has a people upon it like that. That is the true Church of Christ and

He will acknowledge no other." And Dr Whyte concludes by quoting the famous text in Malachi 3:16-17—"Then they that feared the Lord spake often one to another; and the Lord hearkened and heard it, and a book of remembrance was written before him for them that feared the Lord, and that thought upon his name. And they shall be mine, saith the Lord of Hosts, in that day when I make up my jewels; and I will spare them, as a man spareth his own son that serveth him."

It was some while before John came into the full assurance of saving faith. He was going through a period of introspection and retrospection that kept him in an unsettled state, largely the result, no doubt, of contact with Puritan preachers and soldiers in the army. Texts torn from their contexts, doubts, voices, hopes, fears formed a "miry slough" through which he waded. He could never have written as he did years later had he not himself experienced the spiritual conflicts through which his pilgrims had to go.

The immediate effect of the conversation of the women that he heard was to make him distrust his apparent religious condition. This was all to the good, for self-deception is a bondage that still keeps many from knowing the saving grace of Christ. He realised that he had never thought before of the absolute necessity of the new birth; nor did he know the comfort and promises of the Word of God; still less did he know the deceitfulness and treachery of his own wicked heart. "As for my secret thoughts, I took no notice of them."

But he thought much of what he had heard and contrived to go again and again to that part of Bedford in the hope of hearing them talk of the things of God again. "I could not stay away," he tells us. All unknown to himself the grace of God was at work in his heart. He became constrained by the Scriptures they quoted, meditated on them, so that, as he says, "my mind was fixed on Eternity." The Bible became precious to him. He even began to read the letters of Paul.

One day he met in a country lane an old acquaintance of

his named Harry, who when asked how he was, replied that he was well, followed by an outburst of profane oaths. John, who himself used to talk like this, was genuinely shocked. "But Harry," he said, "why do you curse and swear so? What will become of you if you die in this condition?" Harry looked at his former companion in vice with anger and contempt. "Why, what would the devil do for company", he shrugged, "if it were not for such as I?" This encounter, too, made an impact on his soul.

In his travelling among the villages he came upon some people who belonged to the sect called Ranters, loose and shallow sectarians, antinomian in doctrine; but he found no comfort or wisdom in their fanatical notions. Then, one day as he walked from Elstow to Bedford, the idea came to him to test whether he had faith or no. There were many puddles on the road—why not tell the puddles to be dry, and the dry places puddles? But he did not think that he could pray about it, and this discouraged him from the attempt.

Strangely the waves of spiritual conflict surged and swelled, ebbed and flowed. He gained more and more light from the Bedford women members of Mr Gifford's Church. His powerful imagination presented them in a kind of vision, as if they lived in the pleasant warmth on the sunny side of a high mountain, while he was shivering and shrinking in the cold, afflicted with frost, snow, and dark clouds. But a great wall stood between them and himself, which he greatly desired to pass so that he might join them. He began to realise that he had been trying to change and develop his character into that of a saved child of God, and had not till now realised the need of supernatural power and heavenly grace to do it for him. He wanted what they had. He remembered that the Puritan preachers made much of the "effectual call" of Christ to folk to come to him in faith. He longed for Christ to say to him, "Follow me." "I cannot now express," he was to write long afterwards, "with what longings and breakings in my soul I cried to Christ to call me. Thus I continued for a time, all on a flame to be converted to Jesus Christ ... How lovely now was everyone in my eyes that I thought to be converted men and women! They shone, they walked like people that carried the broad seal of Heaven about them."

2

Then he did the sensible thing and told the godly women of Bedford that he too longed for the new birth. They in turn, very wisely introduced him to their pastor John Gifford, who became to John Bunyan both his Evangelist and his Interpreter. They could not have done better, for Gifford himself had had a narrow escape from the City of Destruction, and this was now to be John's experience also.

John Gifford is easily the most arresting character in the Bunyan story, apart from Bunyan himself. He had had a strange career. On the 1st June 1648 a very bitter fight was fought at Maidstone in Kent in a rain-storm, between the Parliamentary forces under Fairfax and a Royalist body, making insurrection in a lost cause on behalf of Charles. Sir Thomas Fairfax never performed a more brilliant exploit than when on that one memorable night at Maidstone the Royalist insurrection was stamped out and extinguished in its own blood. Hundreds of dead bodies filled the streets of the town, hundreds of the enemy were taken prisoners, while hundreds more hid in the hop-fields and woods around the town only to fall into Fairfax's hands the next morning. Among the prisoners was John Gifford, a Royalist major of dragoons, a Kentish man of good family, but known as a fierce and notorious swashbuckler. He had been a leader in the Maidstone uprising and was one of the very few prisoners condemned to death. On the night before his execution, by the courtesy of Fairfax himself, Gifford's sister was permitted to visit her brother in prison. The guards were overcome by weariness and drink and lay heavily asleep; Gifford's sister urged him to escape, and showed him the door to freedom. He got clear away without discovery. For three days he lay in hiding in a ditch, and when the hue and cry after him had died down, he went in disguise to London, and thence to the shelter of some friends of his at Bedford.

Here he married and settled down to the practice of medicine which he had studied before he entered the army.

Gifford had been a dissolute man as a soldier and he became a still more scandalously dissolute man as a civilian. He spent much time with the wine cup and the dice-box. His hatred and opposition to the Puritans of Bedford made his name an infamy and a fear. He reduced himself almost to beggary with gambling and drink, and when near suicide God laid mighty hold upon him and he came under the power of the truth. In the providence of God there came into his hands a Puritan book by John Bolton, *The Four Last Things: Death, Judgement, Hell and Heaven*, published in 1633. The Bedford Church Book records it thus: "Something therein took hold upon him and brought him into a great sense of shame, wherein he continued for ye space of a moneth or above. But at last God did so plentifully discover to him by His word the forgiveness of his sins for the sake of Christ, that (as he hath by severall of the brethren been heard to say) all his life after, which was about ye space of five yeares he lost not the light of God's countenance." Converted he surely was, and his changed life was apparent to all who knew him. In a very short time he was in fellowship with the leading Puritans of Bedford. His talents could not be hid, and before long he was exhorting the saints at meetings in their homes, organising them into a spiritual society, and then becoming their minister and gathering a sizeable congregation drawn from the town and surrounding villages.

Very soon, wonder upon wonders, John Gifford was actually appointed parish minister of St John's Church, Bedford, under Cromwell's evangelical but otherwise inclusive ecclesiastical establishment. Oliver Cromwell, though a strict Calvinist himself, was extremely tolerant of all forms of Christianity except episcopacy and papacy. Any peaceable Christian, he insisted, was entitled to liberty of worship as he thought fit. He sought to establish one Church in which all true believers could worship. In his State Church the parish clergy might have been Presbyterians, Independents, Baptists, or even former Episcopalians who accepted the new situation. During the Interregnum about two thousand clergy out of nine thousand parishes in the country gave up their benefices, so that a substantial majority of English clergy carried on as usual—as Christopher Hall at Elstow did. Under Cromwell two sets of officials governed Church leadership: there were Triers, godly ministers who had to examine new incumbents; and there were Ejectors, prominent local Puritan citizens with local knowledge, who could deprive them of their benefices if they neglected their duties or led immoral lives.

As Lord Protector, Dr Maurice Ashley reminds us, Cromwell maintained the system of paying clergy out of tithes and he allowed lay patrons to appoint parish clergy. It was in this way, through the commendation of leading Puritan citizens of Bedford, that John Gifford was appointed parish minister of St John's. Cromwell's inclusive Church Establishment might be the scorn of the prelatic party, but it was a genuine attempt to obtain order in the Church, without enforcing restricting regulations regarding, for example, the administration of baptism. He would have liked to make the National Church the comprehensive Church that his friend Dr John Owen sought. But Cromwell did not live long enough to see this come about. The Roman Catholic sympathies of both Charles II and James II were decisive against such a system: during their reigns Nonconformists looked back to the Cromwellian Protectorate as a golden age of liberty and peace.

So in 1653 Cromwell's Commissioners, satisfied that John Gifford had the root of the matter in him, appointed the ex-major to the sequestrated living of St John's, Bedford. The Bedford dissenting congregation had been founded in 1650 with some of the leading citizens, including an ex-Mayor, belonging to it. When Gifford became their Pastor at the small Church of St John's, as the Church Book records: "They made choice of Brother Gifford to be their Pastor, or elder, to minister to them the things of the Kingdom of God, to whom they had given themselves before; wherefore Brother Gifford accepted of the charge and gave himself up to the Lord and to His people, to walk with them, watch over them, and dispense the mysteries of the Gospel among them."

The Church thus reformed by him consisted of twelve members "in the Congregational way". Their principal of union was stated as follows: "Now the principle upon which they thus entered into fellowship one with another, and upon which they did afterwards receive those that were added to their body and fellowship, was Faith in Christ and Holiness of life, without respect to this or that circumstance or opinion in outward and circumstantial things. By which means grace and faith was encouraged, love and amity maintained, disputings and occasion to janglings and unprofitable questions avoided, and many that were weak in the faith confirmed in the blessing of eternal life." It was this simple principle of church unity that so influenced John Bunyan and moulded his own views of church fellowship and the sacraments in days to come. This remarkable Church still exists in Bedford, proud of its association with John Gifford and John Bunyan.

3

Brother Gifford, or "holy Mr Gifford" as Bunyan calls him, invited John to St John's rectory for conversation, and there in his spacious garden, he opened up to the troubled tinker the way of salvation—repentance towards God and faith in the Lord Jesus Christ. Lovingly, patiently, and clearly he did it, and Bunyan's burden was slowly lifted and his guilty conscience healed as he drank in the spiritual truths Gifford showed him in private talk and public exhortation. Eagerly Bunyan attended Gifford's ministry at St John's. One sermon by Gifford on a text from the "Song of Songs" —"Behold, thou art fair, my love", reminded the hearers that the love of Christ was not , as John was inclined to think, withheld from the tempted and afflicted soul. This promise filled him with so much hope, Bunyan tells us, that he felt he could have spoken of God's mercy to the crows that sat on the ploughed fields. In *Grace Abounding*, paragraph 89, we have John Gifford's sermon outline, and very good it is.

John Bunyan continued for more than a year in a state of spiritual uncertainty. Sometimes a text would lift his soul on high, but a day or so later another text would send him to despair. He was altogether too introspective. In the pages of *Grace Abounding* he sets down at length these spiritual struggles, which we need not further discuss here. Eventually, however, the truth gripped his soul that through the sin-atoning sacrifice of Christ on the cross, and through faith in his finished work for sinners he could be forgiven and become a true child of God. The text, "He hath made peace by the blood of his cross" was a powerful message to his soul. He received Christ as his Saviour in true repentance for sin, and simple faith and promised obedience, and his struggles were over. In the process he came across a tattered copy of Luther's *Commentary on the Epistle of St Paul to the Galatians*, in a shop, which he bought and carried home to study. It was so old that it almost fell to pieces in his hand. It was greatly to his enlightening and strengthening, for Martin Luther had known spiritual struggles similar to his own. "I do prefer this book of Martin Luther upon the Galatians," he tells us, "(excepting the Holy Bible) before all the books that ever I have seen, as most fit for a wounded conscience."

John Bunyan was formally received into the Puritan Church at Bedford worshipping in St John's Church, in 1653. He was still living at Elstow, but had been attending Gifford's ministry since 1651. Some biographers, who should have known better, boldly stated that Bunyan joined the Baptist Church at Bedford. This is a mistake. There was no Baptist Church in Bedford in 1653 or for many years afterwards. Gifford's church fellowship, as we have seen, was a Union Church, comprising both Congregational and Baptist members. Tradition has it that Gifford baptized John Bunyan one dark night by immersion in the river Ouse, and a place is pointed out where baptizing later on took place. It is indeed possible, but there is no record of this happening, and John himself never mentions it. Only twice between 1650 and

1690 is baptism mentioned in the Church Book of Bedford Meeting, and neither of these is of John Bunyan. At any time between his conversion and his death he would have denied that he was a Baptist—or Anabaptist as the denomination was then known. In his attitude to baptism and other forms of ritual he was deeply influenced by the principles of John Gifford his pastor, and later by those of his friend William Dell who would have abandoned baptism altogether. Writing a farewell letter to the Bedford Church a little before he died John Gifford clearly warned them to avoid "separation from the Church about baptisme, laying on of hands, Anoynting with Oyls, Psalmes, or any externalls". He urged them instead to concentrate on the fundamental truths of the faith. Baptism, he considered, was not one of these. Nor was it to John Bunyan. He did not "preach up" baptism of believers by immersion, as some did in his day, and some do today. Indeed, he was to engage in controversy with some London Baptists of the stricter sort. Towards the end of his book, *A Confession of my Faith* he dealt briefly with the terms on which Christians should be admitted to Communion. He deplores undue attention being given to questions of ritual, "taking off Christians from the more mighty things of God, and to make them quarrel and have heart-burnings one against another."

This tolerance exposed him to a violent attack by three leaders of the more rigid type of London Baptist, William Kiffin, and two colleagues Paul and D'Anvers. He replied to them in 1673 in *Differences in Judgement about Water Baptism no Bar to Communion*. "I dare not say," he wrote, "No matter whether water-baptism be practised or not'. But it is not a stone in the foundation of a church ... The saint is a saint before, and may walk with God, and be faithful with the saints, and to his own light also, although he never be baptised ... I am for communion with saints because they are saints; show me the man that is a visible believer, and although he differ with me about baptism, the doors of the church stand open for him." And he is resolved to have nothing to do with the nomenclature of the sects. "I must tell you, I know none to whom that title (Baptist) is so proper as to the disciples of John. And since you would know by what name I would be distinguished from others, I tell you I would be, and I hope I am, a CHRISTIAN, and choose, if God should count me worthy, to be called a Christian, a Believer, or other such name as is approved by the Holy Ghost. And as for those factious titles of Anabaptists, Independents, Presbyterians, or the like, I conclude that they came neither from Jerusalem nor Antioch (where disciples were first called Christians) but from Hell and Babylon, for they naturally tend to divisions." This was always John Bunyan's position. He was non-sectarian and Evangelical in the best sense.

The members of the Bedford Church joined in fellowship on the principle of "faith in Christ and holiness of life, without respect to this or that circumstance or opinion in outward and circumstantial things." This was ever Bunyan's rule and practice concerning church membership.

4

In 1654 when blind Mary was nearly four years old, a second daughter Elizabeth was born at Elstow, and was christened and registered at the Abbey Church. John seems to have made no objection to infant baptism. A year later he removed his family to a cottage in the parish of St Cuthbert's in Bedford, so that he could more easily attend the ministry of John Gifford. It was a modest house with a gabled roof above the door, with two small living rooms on either side of it, and bedrooms above. The small room on the right became known as "Bunyan's Parlour", and the upper bar of the grate was a steelyard inscribed with the initials "J.B.".

John Gifford was pastor of the Bedford congregation for nearly five years. He had a remarkable influence as a preacher, and throngs of people from villages round about Bedford attended his ministry. Many villagers of Elstow, seeing the difference in John Bunyan's heart and life also began to frequent St John's. Gifford died in 1655, and was buried in the churchyard of St John's, although no stone marks the spot. He was greatly mourned by many in the town of Bedford and the surrounding area. He was a true Mr Great-heart and a Valiant-for-Truth. And to lead John Bunyan to true faith in Christ was a work for which the world-wide Church of God should be abundantly thankful.

John Bunyan, by God's grace, has now left the City of Destruction and is firmly set on the pilgrim highway of spiritual life that leads to the Celestial City. But many are to be his trials and frustrations, as well as his joys and triumphs, before he safely reaches his goal.

6

Puritan Preacher

1

Like his own Christian John Bunyan lost the guilt and burden of his sin at the cross of Christ, and was ‘‘glad and lightsome, and said with a merry heart, He hath given me rest by His sorrows, and life by His death.’’ Bunyan’s own spiritual experiences, together with the characters he met on his pilgrim way, he carefully records in *The Pilgrim’s Progress*. And the classic passage of Christian at the Cross, losing his burden, being enriched with heavenly gifts, receiving the assurance of salvation, was surely his also. ‘‘Then he stood still awhile, to look and wonder; for it was very surprising to him that the sight of the Cross should thus ease him of his burden, He looked therefore, and looked again even till the springs that were in his head sent the waters down his cheeks.’’ At this point three shining ones, evidently angels, come to Christian greeting him with ‘‘Peace be to thee.’’ Bunyan had long sought and longed for peace with God, now he had received it. The first assured him, ‘‘Thy sins be forgiven’’, and for John with his long drawn-out spiritual struggles it was a relief to know that the crucified one had dealt with and removed the guilt and power of sin. The second shining one ‘‘stript him of his rags, and cloathed him with change of raiment". By this he would have us understand that he had received the robe of the righteousness of Christ imputed to him, instead of the filthy rags of his own self-effort and fancied merit. "The third," Bunyan proceeds, "also set a mark on his forehead, and gave him a roll with a seal upon it, which he bade him look on as he ran, and that he should give it in at the Celestial Gate." Many writers have a wrong interpretation of this passage, imagining that the roll was the Bible. The truth is that the roll was Assurance, the assurance of acceptance with God through faith in the Redeemer. And the seal upon it was the gift of the Holy Spirit. Several times did Christian on his pilgrim journey lose his roll, his sense of assurance, but as often as he re-discovered it and pondered it he was strengthened and refreshed for the journey. "Then Christian gave three leaps for joy, and went on singing." No trace of the gloomy, perverse Puritan here. The burden of his song is—

> Blest Cross! blest Sepulchre! blest rather be
> The Man that there was put to shame for me.

Bunyan's Christian faith and knowledge of the Scriptures increased steadily. He grew in grace and in holiness of life. The Independent congregation meeting in St John's Church had weekly meetings for prayer and Bible study as well as the Sunday services. John was to be identified with them for thirty-five years, and to be their pastor for seventeen years, although as yet he did not know it. The Church kept regular minutes of their proceedings in a Church Book between the years 1656 and 1672, days of great stress and strain for Nonconformists, and we shall note Bunyan's part in its affairs in due course. His name stands nineteenth in the list of members. He formed many lasting friendships among the saints at St John's, who not only helped him onward and upward in the Christian life, but in days of dire necessity provided him and his family with practical support also. The Church minutes record the acceptance of converts, the visiting of prisoners in the County Gaol, dealing with delinquent members, and seeking God's guidance in national troubles.

Bedford, in John's time, consisted of five parishes with a total population of about two thousand. Many of the houses were roofed with thatch. There was a strongly exclusive spirit in the civic affairs of the town; natives from other parts of the country were not admitted to the merchant-guild; no resident was permitted to let his house to such a "foreigner" without consent of the Mayor (the only exceptions were the Huguenots after the revocation of the Edict of Nantes in 1685); no innkeeper could house a stranger for more than eight days without reporting him to the Mayor; between ten at night and five in the morning traffic over the bridge was stopped. The streets were ill-paved where paved at all, and street lighting was practically non-existent. The town was almost completely divided by the river Ouse, the two parts being linked by a stone bridge.

The incumbency of St John's remained vacant for several months after the death of John Gifford. The Bedford Council wished to nominate a certain Mr Hayes of Papworth, but the Church wanted a younger man much beloved of its members, and had set their hearts on having John Burton. The dispute was referred to Cromwell himself, who decided in Burton's favour. John Burton was appointed pastor in January 1656, and in the following May the keeping of regular entries in the Church Book began.

2

By this time a third child had been born to Mary and John; he was named John after his father and was destined to be a member of Bedford Meeting for forty-five years. The leaders of the Church were sure that in the converted tinker they had a recruit of no mean order. "Some of the most notable among the saints with us," he wrote in his autobiography "did perceive that God had counted me worthy to understand something of His will in His holy and blessed Word, and had given me utterance, in some measure, to express what I saw to others for edification." So he was asked to accompany the preaching elders when they went to preach in the villages, and added his testimony or a homily to their sermons. The call to exercise his preaching gift was something of a surprise to him, but soon he was regularly engaged in village preaching. Sometime in 1656 in St John's Church, before the assembled members, John was specifically appointed to the public preaching of the Word, "after some solemn prayer to the Lord with fasting". He was thus set apart, not only to edify believers, but also "to offer the Gospel to those who had not yet received the faith thereof". There was also an inward spiritual urge in him to undertake this work, for he came to realise that the Holy Spirit did not intend that men who had gifts and abilities should bury them in the earth, but stirred them up to exercise their preaching gifts. He himself, with true Christian humility, thought himself most unworthy of such duty, and with much fear and trembling went out to preach the Word in the open air on village greens, in barns, in private houses, and sometimes even in parish churches. Bedfordshire and neighbouring shires are full of traditions of his preaching, and several Congregational and Baptist churches claim to have been founded through his preaching. To his amazement, so powerfully did God use him, that people thronged in hundreds to hear him. No doubt the fact of the remarkable transformation made in him through the grace of God brought them flocking to his services, but there was also his homely eloquence, his pictorial style, his pointed admonitions, and his own passionate sincerity to impress and draw them.

At the end of *Grace Abounding* Bunyan gives "A brief account of the Author's Call to the work of the Ministry". He speaks of his own concern for the souls of his hearers, and how he diligently laboured to find some word from God which would awaken their consciences. In this he was successful, for some were convicted of the greatness of their sin and of their need of new life from Christ. And where could he find "some word from God" but from the Bible? Puritanism was, above all else, a Bible movement. To the Puritan the Bible was in truth the most precious possession that this world affords. His deepest conviction was that reverence for God means reverence for Scripture, and serving God means obeying Scripture. To the Puritan it was the living Word of the living God. "To the Puritan Bible student," says Dr J.I. Packer, "it was God who had uttered the prophecies, recorded the histories, expounded the doctrines, declared the promises, written the visions of which Scripture was made up; and he knew that Scripture must be read, not merely as words which God spoke long ago, but as words which God continues to speak to every reader in every age." John Bunyan knew that God spoke to him in the Bible, and he prayerfully sought messages from it in order to speak as God's ambassador to others. "I preached that I felt," he tells us, "what I smartingly did feel ... I went myself in chains to preach to them in chains; and carried that fire in my conscience that I persuaded them to beware of."

3

In two telling paragraphs, 278 and 279 of *Grace Abounding* Bunyan tells us the subject matter of his early sermons. To begin with, "I went for the space of two years, crying out against men's sins, and their fearful state because of them." This was standard Puritan practice, and indeed standard evangelical practice at all times. The Lord Jesus began his public ministry with the words, "Repent ye, and believe the Gospel." Bunyan preached the law of God against sin, and the exceeding sinfulness of sin. The puritan preacher knew that if he did not preach about sin and God's judgements upon it, then he could not present Christ as the Saviour from sin and the wrath of God. We should learn from the Puritans to put first things first in our preaching. If we are silent about sin and God's hatred and punishment of sin, and if we preach a Christ who saves only from self and the sorrows of the world we are not preaching the Christ of the Bible. So much modern preaching appears to consist of half-truths about salvation, and does not go to the root of the matter—man fallen, with a sinful nature, who cannot deliver himself or put himself right with God, but who needs the divine power of the supernatural Saviour to cleanse and deliver him from all sin. If the ten commandments were plainly set before men, women and children, we should not have the crime rate or the permissive society that we endure today. Bunyan goes on, "I should labour so to speak the Word, as that thereby, if it were possible, the sin and the person guilty might be particularized by it." By this he means going into details about particular sins, not making vague statements, but pointing out particular things offensive to a holy God—unbelief, hatred of God's law, evil desires, impure ways, selfishness, greed, hatred, jealousy etc. This was one great characteristic of Puritan preaching, and it stirred up consciences to repent and seek deliverance.

Bunyan next tells us that as he went on in the Christian life and in Gospel preaching, he made many discoveries of the peace and comfort Christ gives. "Wherefore now I altered in my preaching (for still I preached what I saw and felt); now therefore I did much labour to hold forth Jesus Christ in all His Offices, Relations, and Benefits unto the world." He still preached the necessity of salvation from sin, but now he emphasised more than formerly the all-sufficiency of Christ as Lord as well as Redeemer. The constant study of the Bible taught him about Christ as Prophet, Priest, and King; of his power as Shepherd, Vine, and Keeper; of his being Friend and Guide; of Christ as the Way, the Truth, and the Life; in truth as the answer to man's every need, and the power to enable him to live a holy life.

"After this," Bunyan says, "God led me into something of the mystery of union with Christ." By this he means that true faith in the Saviour and obedience to his word, unites the believer with Christ, so that he abides in Christ and Christ abides in him. This faith-union brings into being the graces of a Christ-like character, love, dependence and obedience, and their expression in outward work and service for God and his people.

4

We may well ponder the emphases of Puritan preaching. They diagnosed the plight of man as guilty of sin, polluted by sin, and in bondage to sin; the state of being wholly dominated by an inbred attitude of enmity against God. They stressed man's utter inability to improve himself in God's sight. They declared God's wrath against sin, but his saving love for sinners. Through the sin-atoning work of the Saviour upon Calvary's Cross, the vilest offender against God could be reconciled to him, forgiven and remade, upon repentance towards God and faith in the Lord Jesus Christ. They stressed also the condescension of Christ. He was never less to them than the divine Son of God incarnate, and they measured his mercy by his majesty. They magnified the love of the cross by showing the greatness of the glory which Christ left for it. And they dwelt upon the omnipotence of his grace to conquer subdue and transform rebellious hearts, and his patience and forbearance in his invitations to sinners to come to him and be healed and blessed.

In our day Christians have been appalled to see Anglican theologians, holding important university teaching posts, publish a book entitled *The Myth of God Incarnate*, in which the eternal Son of God is reduced to a mere man like ourselves, and thereby his unique person, teaching, and saving work are nullified and rejected. The scepticism of these Unitarian heretics neither rebuked nor dismissed by their church authorities, contrasts strongly with the vigorous faith of the unlettered tinker of Bedford. Bunyan was no mean controversialist as we shall see, and his knowledge of the Scriptures and of the Lord and his saving work would have demolished such pitiful and unscriptural arguments.

For him, the faith was not a matter of the intellect alone. "I have been," he remarks, "in my preaching, especially when I have been engaged in the doctrine of Life by Christ without works, as if an angel of God had stood by at my back to encourage me. Oh, it had been with such power and heavenly evidence upon my own soul, while I have been labouring to unfold it, to demonstrate it, and to fasten it upon the conscience of others, that I could not be contented with saying, 'I believe and am sure' methought I was more than sure that those things which then I asserted were true."

The Puritan view was that preaching Christ meant teaching the whole Christian system, the character of God, the Trinity, the plan of salvation, the entire work of grace in regeneration and sanctification. Puritan Gospel preaching was above all concerned to honour Christ, to show his glory to needy men and women. And this John Bunyan assuredly did with all his heart.

Bunyan appears to have been appointed a deacon of the Church in 1657, His preaching abilities increased, but his work as a brazier does not appear to have suffered. He is heard preaching the Gospel at Pavenham, Eaton, Gamlingay, Stevington, Ridgmont and other villages near at hand. One wonders whether his father Thomas, that zealous supporter of the Established Church, went to hear him and what he thought of it all. We have no means of knowing. On horseback John often crossed the county borders of Cambridge, Hertford, Buckingham and Huntingdon, and in all these counties are numerous traditions of his preaching visits. At Ridgmont, which was the home of Colonel John Okey, a noted Parliamentary commander, he preached in the small, square-towered Church. On a May morning he preached in a large tithe-barn at Toft, a village west of Cambridge. At the end of the sermon Thomas Smith, the learned Professor of Arabic at Cambridge, told him that he lacked charity in describing his congregation as unbelievers. John, as was his wont, entered into dispute with him on the fallen nature of man. Smith countered with a denial of the tinker's right to preach, to which John replied that God himself and his congregation had called him to the work.

He had another encounter with a University don at Melbourne near Cambridge, but with a happier result. This man, seeing the crowds gathering, stayed "to hear the tinker prate". He stayed to some purpose, for the Word of God gripped him and he was converted. He was William Bedford, who in years to come left the Anglican Church and founded the Congregational Meeting at Royston.

Another Professor, meeting John on a country road near Cambridge, enquired how he dared to preach, not having the original Scriptures.

"Have *you* the originals," asked John, "the actual copies written by the prophets and apostles?"

"No," was the reply, "but I have what I know to be true copies."

"And I," answered John, "believe the English Bible to be a true copy also."

One day in December 1657 John went to Eaton to preach. The vicar, the Rev. Thomas Becke had been appointed to St Mary the Virgin by the House of Lords shortly before. He was a staunch Presbyterian, hostile to the Independents, and believing strongly in a well-trained ministry. News of the coming of a tinker to preach in his parish incensed him, and he obtained a legal indictment against Bunyan which was to be heard at the next Bedford assizes. It is doubtful whether there was any legality in this action as the law then stood. John reported the news of his arrest to the Church, and a day was set apart for prayers on his behalf, and concerning the state of the nation. Nothing came of the affair, and it may be surmised that Mr Becke was more concerned to keep an intruder out of his area than to punish the preacher.

5

Some months later, on Christmas Day 1659, John Bunyan found himself in company with an old acquaintance who had now become a firm friend. He had first met William Dell at Newport Pagnell when serving in the army. Dell was a chaplain to the Parliamentary forces and active in preaching to them. It is doubtful if Bunyan at that time was impressed with Puritan doctrine, but later when he was truly converted he was again brought into contact with Dell, probably through Gifford or some of the Bedford Puritan worthies. William Dell had been a student of Emmanuel College,

Cambridge, that stronghold of Puritanism; he was a man of scholarly mind, strongly held opinions, and freely expressed speech. In 1642 he was appointed Rector of Yeldon, near the Bedfordshire-Northamptonshire border, and amongst his congregation were the Earl and Countess of Bolingbroke who greatly appreciated his ministry. It was through this connection that Dell became well-known to the Commonwealth leaders. In 1645-46 he was chaplain in Fairfax's army at Newport Pagnell. In 1649 he was appointed Master of Gonville and Caius College, Cambridge, a post he held while still Vicar of Yeldon. He wrote a number of Calvinist type theological works, including *Christ's Spirit a Christian's Strength*, and *Right Reformation*. He believed that "all churches are equal as well as all Christians, all being daughters of one mother, beams of one sun, branches of one vine." He also believed in dispensing with baptism altogether as not being an essential part of the Gospel. High in the confidence of the Commonwealth leaders he officiated at the marriage of Cromwell's daughter Bridget to General Ireton in 1646. He was one of the Puritans who offered his services to Charles I on his being sentenced to death, and that unhappy monarch sent him a grateful message: "The king sent him thanks for his love of his soul, hoping that he would be mindful of him in his addresses to God, but as he had made choice of Dr. Juxon he would have no other." Dell was a man of tolerant sympathies and there is little doubt that John Bunyan owed much to him.

Now he rode over to Yeldon to preach a Christmas sermon. William Dell began the service with extempore prayer and reading the Scriptures and then after the singing of a psalm John mounted the narrow oaken stairs of the fifteenth century pulpit. It is a pity that we have no account of this utterance, gladly received by some, gloomily heard by others. After service John joined the Dell family at dinner—one of the daughters being named Mercy, a character whom John was to delineate in *Pilgrim's Progress*. After dinner the two men discussed the unhappy state of the nation. The Lord Protector, Oliver Cromwell, had died in September 1658, worn out before his work was completed, leaving his son Richard as his successor. But Richard's government began to crumble almost immediately. He had never been actively interested in politics, and unlike his brothers had taken no part in the Civil Wars. Richard, nicknamed "Tumbledown Dick", resigned, and the struggle between Army and Parliament produced confusion near anarchy. Dell, who was twenty years older than Bunyan, and a scholar of long experience, expressed his opinion that the anarchy would be put down and the monarchy restored. All the hopes and liberties of the Puritans were likely to be swept away, and the old absolutism in government and repression of Nonconformists would return. Men such as they must prepare for this state of things, and above all else, in the strength of the Lord, remain steadfast to their religious and civil principles.

In June 1660 some of Dell's discontented parishioners sent a petition against him to the House of Lords, in whose archives it is still to be seen. "He has for twelve years past neglected the due administration of the Sacraments, in consequence of which many children were unbaptized ... upon Christmas Day last one Bunyon a tinker was countenanced and suffered to speak in the pulpit to the congregation and no orthodox minister did officiate in the church that day. Since the restoration of the secluded members of Parliament he (Dell) hath declared that the power was now in the hands of the wicked, and that the land was like to be overflowed again with Popery, he hath put forth various seditious books ..." This clearly shows the kind of venom soon to gather force against the Puritans. The petition was dismissed by the House of Lords, rather surprisingly in view of the return of Charles II. But William Dell's days at Yeldon were numbered as he had foreseen. In 1662 after the passing of the Act of Uniformity Dell was ejected from his living and retired to Westoning on his own estate at Samsell, near where John Bunyan was to be arrested, and he died there in 1669, a true man of God and a wise and faithful friend of Bunyan.

6

By the end of 1658 another son, Thomas, had been born to Mary and John Bunyan. Soon afterwards, to his great grief his wife Mary died, and so before he was thirty John was left with four young children, one of them a baby and including his beloved but blind Mary. No doubt he took counsel with the saints at St John's as to what to do in the circumstances, and paid particular attention to the advice of his pastor, John Burton. They recommended him to seek another wife from the Lord to be a mother to his children This, after a short interval and much prayer, he did. His second wife was named Elizabeth, but strangely enough we have no record of the marriage, and like his first wife we do not even know her surname or where she came from. Like Mary, Elizabeth never became a member of the Independent Church to which her husband belonged, and from this fact we may suppose that she remained loyal to the Church of England. She was much younger than John, but a more loyal and loving helpmeet he could not have had, caring for the children with the utmost affection and standing by her husband when dark troubles swept over the nation and her own family.

7

In the early days of his preaching John Bunyan had many encounters with the sect called "Quakers". Today, the Society of Friends are known for their testimony against the unlawfulness of war, and their concern for social righteousness in all departments of life. But their modern quietism is far removed from the turbulent and pugnacious activities of their early days. They were the most fanatical of sects. They showed no respect for authority in Church or State. It was a common occurrence with them to interrupt worship in "the steeple house" as they called it, and to denounce the proceedings of prayer and praise as empty and unspiritual forms, and even to shout insults at the Minister by such terms as Hireling, Deceiver, False Prophet, and Dog!

Richard Baxter was thus insulted, and many of the Puritan preachers also. Not infrequently some of them would walk or ride naked into a town as a prophetical act. At Bristol, one of them, James Naylor, accompanied by a small procession of women, rode into the town as the Messiah. Their doctrine of the "inner light" was carried to extremes by many, some of whom including George Fox the founder of the movement, and Edward Burrough often urged their hearers to throw away their Bibles and give heed to the light within. To orthodox Puritans like John Bunyan this was dreadful and dangerous doctrine; the "inner light" being vague and unreliable, while the Bible was the inspired Word of God, concrete and infallible. When a certain Quaker, Anne Blackley, urged him publicly to "throw away the Scriptures", he calmly replied, "No, for then the devil would be too hard for me." Oliver Cromwell himself seems to have treated them with toleration so long as they obeyed the law, and even had friendly conversation with George Fox. But most Puritans regarded the Quakers as fanatical and anti-Christ.

In 1654 John Crook, a county magistrate and member of the Little Parliament, had been converted to Quakerism and turned his estate, Beckring's Park, between Ampthill and Woburn into a stronghold of the Society of Friends. From this place individual Friends, or companies of them, made their way to Bedford where they interrupted meetings and services and generally made themselves obnoxious to the peaceable citizens. They emphasised the "power of Christ within", and denounced all worship and religious practices not in accordance with their notions. John Bunyan was many times interrupted in his preaching, and came to regard the Quakers as heretics, rejecting the inspired Word of God, and the historic facts of the Christian faith. One clash between him and Quakers occurred in the High Street at the market cross, where John often stood to offer Christ freely as the only Redeemer of sinners. On another occasion at a meeting at Pavenham his message was strongly opposed by a group of Quakers. And at St Paul's Church, Bedford, on 23rd May

1656 John Bunyan and John Burton his Pastor engaged in open debate with the Quakers on the essential points of the Christian faith.

In *Grace Abounding* ten years afterwards, John Bunyan condemns the "errors of the Quakers" and the "vile and abominable things fomented by them". There was reason and justice in his views of them; their errors both in teaching and practice were the direct result of their rejection of the Word of God. Being forced to consider their views and methods, because of their recurrent opposition to his Gospel preaching, led him into his very first attempt at authorship, and thus to becoming one of the foremost "English men of letters". The work was an answer to the teaching of the Quakers and was entitled, *Some Gospel Truths Opened, according to the Scriptures, or the Divine and Human Nature of Jesus Christ ... Published for the good of God's chosen ones, by that unworthy servant of Christ, John Bunyan of Bedford, by the grace of God, preacher of the Gospel of His dear Son*. The Puritans delighted in long drawn-out titles of their works, aiming at presenting the reader with a full account of the contents. John Burton, Pastor of the Bedford Church, contributed an Introduction in which he wrote that the tinker-author was "not chosen out of an earthly but out of an heavenly university, where he had through grace taken these three degrees—to wit, union with Christ, the anointing of the Spirit, and experience of the temptations of Satan, which do more fit a man for that mighty work of preaching than all University learning that can be had."

It was an astonishing work for so young a Christian, showing a knowledge of the Bible and a grasp of essential Christian doctrines that proved beyond doubt that John was a scholar in the school of the Holy Spirit who was showing him the things of Christ, as the Saviour promised that he would. In 216 pages John contended against the Quaker habit of "spiritualizing" the living, literal Jesus, who lived, was crucified and rose again. It is also surprising to see with what a good literary style he sets forth his thesis that the Son of Mary is very God, that he made the world, that he is our

Saviour, that he died for sinners, redeeming his church with his own blood. His style is plain, emphatic, and clearly formed by his constant reading of the Bible. He enlarges on the second coming of Christ, a favourite topic of some Puritan preachers, giving the reasons for it and the signs of it, as he understands the Scriptures to show these. He then urges his readers to examine their hearts to see if they have true faith in Christ, and if they are "born again", setting forth the proofs and evidences of it as he knew them himself. He concludes with "Some questions to the Quakers" on points they disputed with him concerning the divine and human natures of Christ. It is an impressive treatise for a young man of twenty-seven, only three years converted. The book was published in 1656 by J. Wright of London and M. Cowley of Newport Pagnell. Matthias Cowley, his old friend of army days, stationer and bookseller, adding his name to Bunyan's title page, helped to bring his friend's publication to the attention of Bedfordshire readers.

8

John Bunyan's *Gospel Truths Opened* roused the wrath of a fervent young Quaker of twenty-three, Edward Burrough, destined to die for his faith in Newgate Prison, London six years later. He replied in a pamphlet hardly marked by Quaker meekness, entitled, *The True Faith of the Gospel of Peace*, in which he strongly criticised "the professed minister in Bedfordshire", though without effective Scripture backing. John, warming to his task, dealt with Burrough in a further pamphlet, *A Vindication of Gospel Truths Opened, According to the Scriptures*, in which he dealt with Ranters as well as Quakers. In particular he deals with the "inner light" or "Spirit within all men", avowed by Quakers, and he shows it to be contrary to Scripture, This work was also published by J. Wright of London and Matthias Cowley of Newport Pagnell. Burrough replied a second time against "John Bunyan's foule dirty lies and slanders", but Bunyan met this onslaught with dignified silence. His notable skill in defending Gospel truths was one of the factors that later led the members of the Bedford Church to choose him as their pastor.

The encouragement he received from his Bedford friends and those further afield, stirred him to use his pen again shortly afterwards. He had preached a sermon on the parable of the Rich Man and the Beggar in Luke 16, 19-31, and no doubt repeated it on many occasions. He proceeded to publish it, giving it the rather horrific title of *A Few Sighs from Hell, or the Groans of a Damned Soul*. It is a thoughtful verse by verse exposition of the passage in the manner of the time, by one who had himself known the bondage of sin and feared the wrath of God in consequence. He lets his imagination run away with him as he sets forth the terrors of the damned, and the miseries of those in this life who live without Christ; but he is careful to point the way to forgiveness and blessing through faith in the mercy of Christ. In his foreword, "The Author to the Reader" he writes, "I am thine, if thou be not ashamed to own me, because of my low and contemptible descent in the world. John Bunyan." In the second and subsequent editions this was altered to "I am thine to serve in the Lord Jesus."

For this book he asked his friend John Gibbs, vicar of Newport Pagnell, whom he had met in his army days, to write a Preface. He was a Cambridge man and quite young when, in 1646, he was appointed the Puritan Vicar of the garrison town. In 1660, when John Burton's health began to fail, the Bedford Church invited Gibbs and some others to help with the Sunday services. The reason for this was that Gibbs had been ejected from his living at Newport Pagnell for refusing to admit some notorious but influential drunkards to Holy Communion. He had thought of founding an Independent Church in Newport, but meanwhile was very willing to help the Bedford Meeting. He left the vicarage and rented a small cottage at the end of a long yard for fourpence a week. Behind it stood a commodious barn which the Independents soon came to use for their meetings because of its secluded position. The church thus founded was later to have as its

Minister the Rev William Bull, friend of John Newton and William Cowper. George Offer, in his collected edition of Bunyan's works, ascribes the Preface to *A Few Sighs from Hell* to John Gifford, but Gifford had been dead two years when the book was published in 1658. The Preface is signed J.G. and is known to be by John Gibbs.

John Gibbs writes of John Bunyan thus: "Concerning the author (whatsoever the censures and reports of many are) I have this to say, that I verily believe God hath counted him faithful, and put him into the ministry; and though his outward condition and former employment was mean, and his human learning small, yet is he one that hath acquaintance with God, and taught by His Spirit, and hath been used in His hand to do souls good ... you shall find him magnifying and exalting the Holy Scriptures, and largely showing the worth, excellency, and usefulness of them." The phrase "former employment" is curious, and seems to suggest that John had given up the tinker's trade. If this is so he must have been supported by the Bedford Church, many of whose congregation were men of substance, so that he could devote his whole time to preaching the Gospel.

9

But shadows were already gathering over the land and putting fear into many Puritan hearts. General Monck marched his forces from Scotland to end the anarchy in London and to prepare for the Restoration of the monarchy. Many of the Presbyterian leaders had joined with the Royalists to ensure the return of the king, but they were soon to find that, with the Independents, Baptists, Quakers and other nonconformists, they too would know the hand of government oppression upon them. Monck set up the "Convention Parliament", and Charles II issued the Declaration of Breda in which he promised liberty to "tender consciences" and an amnesty for all except those excluded by Parliament, the regicides and others. Clarendon, his chief political adviser, understood much about the governing of a state, but he could not understand the spirit and principles of the Puritans. On May 25th 1660, Charles stepped ashore at Dover, a swarthy, dark-haired, light-hearted man of thirty. The Mayor received him with the gift of an English Bible, which Charles accepted, declaring that "It was the thing that he loved above all things in the world"—possibly the most monstrous lie ever uttered publicly by any monarch in the world! Before the end of the year episcopacy was re-established, and the surviving episcopal clergy returned to their livings from which the Puritans had ousted them. Back in triumph to St Mary's Bedford came Dr Giles Thorne; back to St John's came the aged Theodore Crowley with his assistant Robert Guidot.

In late August the Bedford Church recorded in their Church Book that "the Lord hath taken to Himself our teacher, bro. Burton." More significant, perhaps, they added "We desire our bro. Harrington, bro. Coventon, bro. John ffenne to take care to informe themselves of a convenient place for our meeting so soone as they can (we being now deprived of our former place); and reporte it to ye Church." So the saints of the Bedford Meeting were turned out of St John's, and the stricken community, deprived of both Pastor and meeting place, did not know that for more than twelve years they would be driven into fields, woods, attics and barns before they found an abiding home.

7

Imprisonment

In spite of the threatening shadows cast over Nonconformity by the restoration of the monarchy and episcopacy, there was no little hope in John Bunyan's heart. For one thing had not Charles II solemnly declared that he would grant "liberty to tender consciences"? And John, like thousands of others, believed him. But he was soon to be disillusioned on this point. Another source of hope was that his young wife Elizabeth was pregnant, expecting her first child before Christmas.

1

When he had written *Grace Abounding* Bunyan added a long and surprisingly detailed account of his imprisonment entitled, "A Relation of the Imprisonment of Mr John Bunyan." It is clear that he had an exceptionally good memory, for he recalls conversations and happenings six years earlier with ease. This beginning of sore trials to Bunyan, and of twelve years in prison, held there without proper legal warrant for no other reason than that he refused to conform to episcopacy and its Prayer Book, made him a renowned author and one of the best known and best loved in the world.

On 12th November 1660 John Bunyan had a preaching engagement at a farmhouse at Lower Samsell, near Harlington, thirteen miles from Bedford on the road to Luton. It is unlikely that he walked this long distance but went on horseback. He knew the district well for he had often preached there, out of doors in good weather. When he entered the room where the service was to be held he found his friends waiting for him ill-at-ease and apprehensive. They soon told him the reason. It had come to their knowledge that a warrant was out for his arrest, and some said that the house was being watched. The local magistrate, Mr Francis Wingate, had issued the warrant. There is little doubt that John Bunyan, who was the most prominent Nonconformist preacher in Bedfordshire, was the main target of the returned Anglican royalists who had determined to silence him as an example to the rest.

John was undeterred. His host urged him to give up preaching that day and to make good his escape. John would have none of it. Bible in hand and subject ready in his mind he answered, "No, by no means; I will not stir, neither will I have the meeting dismissed. Come, be of good cheer, let us not be daunted; our cause is good, we need not be ashamed of it, to preach God's Word is so good a work, that we shall be well rewarded if we suffer for that."

Then he calmly walked out into a field to consider his situation more carefully. He realised that the crisis which William Dell and he had foreseen a year ago was now upon them. He was not so much concerned for himself, but for the effect on his brethren if he were to make his escape and hide. They would think that he was not so strong in deed as in word and would be injured in their faith. His flight would also cause the enemies of the Gospel to blaspheme. "I could have been gone about an hour before the officer approached me; but I would not; for I was resolved to see the utmost of what they could say or do unto me." So he went back into the house and commenced the meeting with prayer. Before long a constable appeared, together with a servant of the magistrate, with the warrant. They looked somewhat abashed to see such a peaceful assembly, with no weapons such as they expected, save the sword of the Spirit, the Bible. John was duly arrested. "But before I went away I spoke some few words of counsel and encouragement to the people, declaring to them that they saw we were prevented of our opportunity to speak and hear the Word of God, and were like to suffer for the same: desiring them that they should not be discouraged, for it was a mercy to suffer upon so good an account." John was marched off in custody of the two men, but as the magistrate Francis Wingate was away from his home at Harlington House that day, John was lodged in a friend's house for the night.

2

Next morning he was brought by the village constable before Francis Wingate, who was a typical country gentleman of the day, a Justice of the Peace, and by virtue of this fact practically a judge and a police magistrate. But his jurisdiction in the area was limited and it was fairly easy for offenders to escape into some other district where they would be safe. Nonconformists soon came to make good use of this loop-hole in the law holding their meetings where possible near county boundaries where escape over the border was easy. John Bunyan remembered this possibility when he described the escape of Christian and Hopeful from Giant Despair on the King's Highway, where they "were safe, because they were out of his jurisdiction". Today, however, John had no intention of escaping, but intended to witness for his Lord before any who questioned his proceedings.

Harlington House was an ancient gabled Manor, in part going back to 1396. It had wide, well-kept lawns and flower beds. Charles II himself had quite recently spent a night in the house. John and the constable were taken to the "great parlour", a fine panelled room with full-length windows opening on to the garden. Here, behind his desk, sat Francis Wingate. He questioned the constable closely on what the people at the meeting were doing, where they met, and what they had with them. This was obviously an enquiry as to whether any weapons were to be seen. The constable replied that only a few persons had met together to preach and hear the Word, and there was no sign of anything else. The magistrate was now clearly embarrassed by his precipitous action and hardly knew what to do. So he began to question John Bunyan. What was he doing at the meeting? Why was he not content to follow his trade? Then he concluded with, "It is against the law for such as you to do as you do!"

Calmly John Bunyan replied that the reason for his coming there was to instruct and counsel people to forsake their sins and "close in with Christ, lest they did perish miserably". And he added that he could both follow his calling and preach the Word also. This reply seemed to incense Wingate, who said roughly that he would "break the neck of our meetings". Wingate next demanded sureties, or he would send Bunyan to prison. Two or three of John's friends were on hand to be his sureties that he would duly appear at the next Quarter Sessions, and when the bond was drawn up Wingate warned John and his supporters that if he preached again before the Sessions their bond would be forfeited. John at once released his sponsors from their bond on his behalf, frankly telling Wingate that he would not give up speaking the Word of God.

Francis Wingate retired to another room to draw up the writ called a "mittimus" committing Bunyan to Bedford Gaol. While John waited for this document, still closely guarded by the constable, a relative of Wingate, Dr William Lindall, Vicar of Hitchin, came into the room. John describes him as "an old enemy of the truth". Lindall began to taunt John with many reviling terms and accused him of meddling with that for which he had no warrant, namely preaching. John quoted Peter to him—"As every man hath received the gift, even so let him minister the same." Lindall then made a sneering remark about Bunyan with reference to Alexander the coppersmith, one of Paul's opponents. But John was equal to him and said, "I also have read of very many priests and Pharisees that had their hands in the blood of our Lord Jesus Christ.'' Lindall proceeded to accuse John of being one of those scribes and Pharisees ''With pretence you make long prayers to divide widow's houses.'' ''If you,'' replied John quietly, ''had got no more by preaching and praying than I have done, you would not be so rich as you are now!'' This shot went home. But immediately a text flashed through his mind, ''Answer not a fool according to his folly'', and so he made only brief replies to Lindall's further efforts to goad him.

3

The writ having been drawn up, Bunyan was starting on the journey to Bedford with the constable, when two friends stopped them and offered to intercede with Wingate for his release. Though he was very weary John waited with the constable while the two men went to the house and entered on a lengthy discussion with Wingate. After some time they returned in triumph. If John would say certain words to Francis Wingate he would be released. ''If the words are such that I may say them with a good conscience I will say them,'' he declared, ''otherwise I will not.'' Back to the panelled hall he was taken where, to his surprise, he found not only Wingate, but his brother-in-law, Dr William Foster of Bedford, doctor of laws and a champion of Anglican orthodoxy, who had been foremost in harrying Nonconformists. He greeted Bunyan ''with seeming affection'', but, since he knew the man, this simulated cordiality was lost on John. Foster repeated Wingate's statement, that if he promised not to call people together, he could go home. In the argument about preaching which followed, Bunyan stoutly defended his call from God and said, ''If I come into any place where there is a people met together, I should, according to the best of my skill and wisdom, exhort and counsel them to seek out after the Lord Jesus Christ, for the salvation of their souls.'' The long controversy which is fully recorded in *Grace Abounding*, ended with the deliverance of the writ to the constable; and although some of Wingate's own servants sought to persuade John not to preach and thus land himself in gaol, he was firm in his resolve. So with the constable, and perhaps with his two helpful friends, John stepped out into the cold night air towards Bedford Gaol and twelve years imprisonment. Francis Wingate would have been astonished could he have looked into the future, to see three of his daughters, Frances, Anna and Rachel, members of the very church in Bedford of which Bunyan was a member and of which he was to become Minister.

"It is not generally remembered," writes Dr Stoughton in his book, *Church of the Restoration*, "that long before the Uniformity, Conventicle and Five Mile Acts were passed, John Bunyan was cast into Bedford Gaol." The fact is that there were still on the Statute Book, unrepealed, acts of relentless severity enforcing conformity with the Established Church. The old Statute Law, 1 Eliz.c.2 required all persons to resort to Church every Sunday and holy day, or be fined and publicly censured. Another law, 35 Eliz.c.1. made frequenting conventicles punishable by imprisonment: those who after conviction would not submit were to be banished the realm. It was under these Acts, within six months of the king's arrival, and long before the legislation known as the Clarendon Code was enacted, that the warrant was issued for John Bunyan's arrest and the writ for his committal to prison.

4

The prison which, with a brief interval in 1666, was to be his enforced home for the next twelve years, carrying "God's comfort in his poor soul", was the County Gaol at the corner of Silver Street and High Street in Bedford. A widespread error long maintained that he was confined in the town lock-up, an old building picturesquely built on the many-arched bridge over the river Ouse. But this was too small to hold the large numbers of prisoners known to be in gaol with Bunyan; besides which, the bridge with its town lock-up collapsed into the river during a storm in 1671. The fact that Bunyan was held in the County Gaol is confirmed by the discovery in 1934 of many assize records of the Norfolk Circuit. These revealed John Bunyan's name on the list of prisoners in Bedford County Gaol for various years between 1661 and 1672. He was there, and not in the town lock-up, because he was arrested under the warrant of a county magistrate for a county offence, and tried at the Quarter Sessions for the county. There was, as we shall see, a second short imprisonment in the County Gaol in 1677, documents concerning which have also been discovered.

The County Gaol to which John Bunyan came on the 14th of November, 1660 had two floors; the ground floor had two day rooms and several sleeping cells for felons, and the first floor, reserved for debtors, had four lodging rooms and a common day-room used also as a chapel. Below the ground floor were two dungeons, one in total darkness. These rooms had no fireplaces and the prisoners slept on straw. It must have been intensely cold for them in winter. There was a small yard behind the building, used as an exercise place. Windows with iron gratings on Silver Street allowed prisoners to hang purses out of the windows on Sunday mornings, begging help from passers-by. Sanitation was primitive. Food was poor, and when more Nonconformists crowded the place, often insufficient. Yet the prison was no worse than hundreds of others throughout the land.

The news of John's arrest caused consternation to the members of the Bedford Meeting. An attempt was made to enlist the help of an Elstow magistrate named Crompton, who probably knew John well, but although sympathetic he was deterred from doing anything because the writ stated only that John had attended conventicles "to the great disparagement of the government of the Church of England", and Crompton suspected that some political offence had been committed.

Consternation was also caused to his wife Elizabeth, near to her first confinement, who went into premature labour and gave birth to a still-born child, a great sorrow to them both. When sufficiently recovered she often came to the prison bringing food and hot soup in an earthen jug, (which is still to be seen at Bunyan Meeting) and other comforts to John.

5

The Quarter Sessions were held in January 1661, and as Bedford did not possess an Assize Court, the Sessions were held in an ancient Gothic semi-ecclesiastical building known as the Chapel of Herne on the bank of the Ouse. A few days earlier there had been a violent uprising of Fifth Monarchy men in London led by a fanatical cooper, Thomas Venner, much influenced by the writings of John Lilburne. This uprising was suppressed with the utmost rigour, many were killed or taken prisoner, and Venner and ten others executed. Those involved in Bunyan's trial, therefore, were likely to be prejudiced against him by these events, which to ignorant minds were no different from other Nonconformist activities. Further, on January 10th a proclamation was made prohibiting "all unlawful and seditious meetings and conventicles under pretence of religious worship". As a result many Dissenters were thrown into prison until the Coronation.

The bench, before which Bunyan appeared, consisted of five County magistrates, three of whom had old scores to pay off against the Puritans. These were Sir Henry Chester of Liddington, Wingate's uncle; George Blundell of Cardington; and the Chairman of Sessions, Sir John Kelynge. The two remaining magistrates were Justices Beecher and Snagg. Sir John Kelynge was a member of the Inner Temple, a practising barrister, a Sergeant-at-law, and one of the counsel for the crown at the trial of the Regicides. It was not likely that John would get much sympathy from him. His bearing on the bench is said to have been haughty and brutal, and he did not scruple to browbeat, fine and imprison any jury who did not follow his wishes. In addition, and most important, although John did not know it, Kelynge had himself been imprisoned by the Commonwealth Government. In 1642 at the Spring Quarter Sessions in

Hertfordshire, he had tried to persuade the Grand Jury to indict certain persons found drilling in connection with the Militia Ordinance. This suggested royalist sympathies. He was summoned to the Bar of the House of Commons, arrested, and imprisoned for sixteen years until the Restoration. To such a man, with his hatred of Puritans and bitter memories of his long imprisonment, John Bunyan must make his pleas. It did not look a very hopeful prospect, nor did it turn out to be.

The Bill of Indictment declared that "John Bunyan, labourer ... hath devilishly and perniciously abstained from coming to Church to hear divine service, and is a common upholder of several unlawful meetings and conventicles, to the great hindrance and distraction of the good subjects of this kingdom." As Vera Brittain points out, "this pompous pronouncement put the small gathering at Lower Samsell right into the picture of the national struggle for freedom of worship." When the clerk asked, "What say you to this?", John replied, "I am a common frequenter of the Church of God, and I am also, by grace, a member with those people over whom Christ is the Head."

"But do you come to church?" asked Kelynge, testily, "You know what I mean, the parish church, to hear divine service?"

"No," answered John, "I do not."

"Why not?"

"Because I do not find it commanded in the Word of God."

"We are commanded to pray," said Kelynge.

"But not by the Common Prayer Book."

"How then?"

"With the Spirit. As the apostle said, 'I will pray with the spirit and with the understanding."

Kelynge retorted, "We may pray with the Spirit, with understanding, and with the Common Prayer Book also."

A long discussion now ensued between John and the magistrates on the nature of prayer and the status of the Prayer Book, all of which is set down in great fulness in Bunyan's

Relation of His Imprisonment, first printed in 1765, and most probably withheld from the press in Bunyan's lifetime because many of the persons concerned were still alive. Kelynge next drew from the prisoner the admission that he was not against the use of the Common Prayer Book so much as against its *compulsory* use. "They that have a mind to use it have their liberty; that is, I would not keep them from it; but for our part, we can pray to God without it". From this subject Kelynge turned to Bunyan's call to preach, and his authority for so doing. Bunyan, from his knowledge of the Scriptures quoted 1 Peter 4:10 and Acts 18. Kelynge, growing impatient, said that he was not so well versed in Scripture as to dispute, and anyway, they could not wait any longer. "You confess the indictment, do you not?" Up to this point John did not know that he was being indicted. The true nature of his interrogation had not been made clear to him. He replied stoutly, "This I confess, we have had many meetings together, both to pray to God, and to exhort one another, and that we had the sweet comforting presence of the Lord among us for our encouragement ... I confessed myself guilty no otherwise."

"Then," thundered Kelynge, "hear your judgement. You must be had back again to prison, and there lie for three months following; and at three months' end, if you do not submit to go to Church to hear divine service, and leave your preaching, you must be banished the realm. And, if after such a day as shall be appointed for you to be gone, you shall be found in this realm, or be found to come over again without special leave from the king, you must stretch by the neck for it, I tell you plainly." And then to the jailor, "Take him away."

So John Bunyan was committed to prison after his court utterances had been regarded as a confession of the indictment. But he was to have the last word. Looking steadily at the five magistrates, he answered Kelynge, "I am at a point with you. If I was out of prison today, I would preach the Gospel again tomorrow, by the help of God!" So he was returned to gaol. But he adds, "I can truly say, I bless the

Lord Jesus Christ for it, that my heart was sweetly refreshed in the time of my examination, and also afterwards at my returning to the prison. So that I found Christ's words more than bare trifles, where He saith, He will give a mouth and wisdom, even such as all the adversaries shall not resist or gainsay. And that His peace no man can take from us."

John Bunyan never forgot his trial at the Quarter Sessions, and sixteen years later he was able to describe the court-house, the proceedings, and give Sir John Kelynge an inglorious immortality as Lord Hategood in Vanity Fair.

It is very likely that John Bunyan as a soldier, impulsive, hot-headed, daring, a born leader of men, had done some deeds of valiant military prowess, for which in our day he might have received a medal. These would he known and he would have been regarded as a hero. Hence, when he came before the judges they would know about his military exploits, which, from their point of view, had been performed on the wrong side. Had he been a soldier in the Royalist army it cannot be doubted that he would have gone free.

For the next three months John remained in prison, chiefly in the company of debtors, vagabonds and criminals. No doubt he spoke to them of the things of God. But soon afterwards he was joined by John Rush, a leading Quaker, and as the days went by other Nonconformists were added to their number. Then on the 3rd of April he received an official visit from Paul Cobb, the Clerk of the Peace, who interviewed him in the gaoler's room. He had come, he said, at the request of the magistrates to admonish him, and to demand his submission to the Church of England. The alternative was that he could be sent away out of England "or else worse than that". He must submit to the laws of the land and leave off the meetings he had been having. John protested that the law under which he was detained did not apply to him, but to those who designed to do evil in their meetings, using religion for a cloak for wickedness. His meetings were solely to worship God and do good to others. Cobb replied that everyone would say the same, and referred to Venner's insurrection in London. John said that he abhorred their practices. "I look upon it as my duty," he affirmed, "to behave myself under the king's government, both as becomes a man and a Christian, and if an occasion was offered me, I should willingly manifest my loyalty to my Prince, both by word and deed." Cobb said that he did not profess to be a man able to dispute, nevertheless he proceeded to argue with Bunyan for a considerable time that the prisoner might exhort small companies of people in private and also attend public worship of the Established Church. He also dropped the hint that John could be sent to Spain or Constantinople or some other remote place. John persisted that he knew no evil that he had done. Cobb reminded him that Scripture said, "The powers that be are ordained of God." John answered that both Jesus and Paul suffered under the ruling powers. "Sir," he concluded, "the law hath provided two ways of obeying: The one to do that which I, in my conscience, do believe that I am bound to do, actively; and where I cannot obey actively, there I am willing to lie down, and to suffer what they shall do unto me." Paul Cobb sat still and gazed at Bunyan as at some fanatic. John thanked him for his "civil and meek discoursing with me". And he added a characteristic touch—"Oh that we might meet in heaven!"

Before we leave Paul Cobb it must be noted that he had a clearer grasp of Bunyan's legal position than Bunyan himself, or indeed some of his biographers. On 10th December 1670, nearly ten years after Bunyan's conviction at the Quarter Sessions, Cobb sent an account of it to Roger Kenyon, Clerk of the Peace for Lancashire, as a guide to procedure in similar cases. This document lay unnoticed among the Kenyon family papers until 1894, but it is important to this history. Paul Cobb wrote as follows: "One Bonyon was indicted upon the Statute of 35 Elizabeth for being at a Conventicle. He was in prison and was brought into Court and the indictment read to him; and because he refused to plead to it, the Court ordered me to record his confession, and he hath lain in prison upon that conviction, ever since

Christmas Sessons, 12 Chas.II. And my Lord Chief Justice Kelynge was then upon the Bench, and gave the rule, and had the like, a year ago, against others. Bonyon hath petitioned all the Judges of Assize, as they came the Circuit, but could never be released. And truly, I think it but reasonable that if any one do appear, and afterwards will not plead, but that you should take judgement by nihil dicit, or confession."

7

By contemporary standards he had received a fair trial, being sentenced to what the existing regulations prescribed, imprisonment until he conformed. He remained in prison because he deliberately broke repressive laws which violated his conscience. Robert Bridges, a former Poet Laureate, a fine poet but a poor judge of character, wrote of John Bunyan in his collected Essays as follows: "Having the choice between silence with imprisonment and silence with freedom, his conscience forced him to prefer the material fetters, and leave his family to the charity of his friends." This is most unjust and proves that Bridges knew nothing of soul experience or remotely understood the problem of conscience. "It is quite untrue to say that his imprisonment was self-inflicted because he would not accept the proffered terms of freedom", writes Vera Brittain, one who really did understand the problem of conscience. "With liberty of worship at the core of his belief, he could not have accepted them. His duty as a Christian was to save not merely his own soul, but the souls of his brethren. Silence with freedom would have violated his conscience, since it would have involved the deliberate choice of silence. For silence imposed on him by the law he was not responsible. No honest man, deeply moved by conviction could, in his circumstance, have chosen personal liberty, whatever the cost of refusing it might be for himself or for others." She goes on to point out that John Bunyan and his fellow Independents were fighting for the right of a Christian to decide, without interference from the State or its Established Church, the character of his relationship to God. He could not renounce a conviction that was essential to his faith in order to preserve his freedom. Many in Germany, Russia and elsewhere have gone to concentration camps rather than stifle the voice of conscience and its expression in word and deed. We need to remember this in days when personal conviction and freedom of speech and assembly are being attacked in many places! And of course Bunyan did not, as Bridges sneered, leave his family to the charity of his friends, as we shall see.

The Coronation of Charles II was on 23rd April 1661 and there was a general expectation of a release of many prisoners as an indication of the king's grace. John Bunyan hoped for release also but although thousands were released, he was not. Apparently John was regarded as a convicted person, as Paul Cobb plainly shows, and in his case he must apply for a pardon and had twelve months in which to do it.

8

The petition presented by John Bunyan, carefully written no doubt with the assistance of leading members of his church better educated than himself, had no effect. There seemed to be an official conspiracy to keep him in prison, and very likely there was. It was thought that a peer, Lord Barkwood, about whom nothing is known, might be sympathetic in the matter and Elizabeth undertook the intimidating journey of two or three days to London to enlist his help. Leaving the children with neighbours she went to London, interviewed Lord Barkwood and presented John's petition for release. He consulted other Lords and then told her that John could be released only by the judges at the next Bedfordshire Assize.

In August 1661 the Midsummer Assize was held at the Chapel of Herne. One of the judges was Sir Matthew Hale, a remarkable man who in 1655 had sat in Cromwell's Parliament, but at the Restoration was made Chief Baron of the Exchequer, and in 1671 became Lord Chief Justice. He was the author of the *History of the Common Law of*

England and other notable legal works. He was also known as one who had sympathy for dissenters, amongst whom he had been educated, and who did his best to mitigate the severity of the law. The other judge was Sir Thomas Twisden, a hard man of conventional outlook, not likely to be helpful.

Elizabeth Bunyan, still very young, but steadfast in her devotion to the faith and to John, presented the petition to Sir Matthew Hale. Says John, "He very mildly received it at her hand, telling her that he would do her and me the best good he could; but he feared, he said, he could do none." Next day, summoning up her courage, she intercepted the coach of Sir Thomas Twisden as he drove through the town and threw a copy of the petition on to his lap. It was a bold but perhaps not very wise thing to do and it made him angry. Stopping the coach he snapped at her that John was a convicted person who could not be released unless he promised to stop preaching.

Undeterred by this rough treatment Elizabeth went to the Chapel of Herne where the Assize was in session and, in an interval of the proceedings, presented the third copy of the petition to Hale. He seemed inclined to consider the matter again, but Sir Henry Chester, one of John's examiners at the previous Sessions, dissuaded him. Then the High Sheriff, Edward Wylde of Houghton Conquest, took her part and drawing her aside urged her to try again after the Assize was over, when, with the local gentry, the Judges met to consider the business of the County in the Swan Chamber.

So to the Swan Chamber, the upper room of the Swan Inn, she went, to make her last endeavour. She was only a young peasant woman without education, means, or influence, yet she stands forth in history as not least among the world's worthies. She addressed Sir Matthew Hale once more. "My Lord, I make bold to come once again to your Lordship to know what may be done with my husband." Sir Matthew was somewhat exasperated. "Woman, I told thee before I could do thee no good." Elizabeth made a spirited reply: "My Lord, he is kept unlawfully in prison; they clapped him up before there was any proclamation against the meetings; the indictment also is false. Besides, they never asked him whether he was guilty or no; neither did he confess the indictment." It was all too true, but from Kelynge's and Cobb's point of view the action was quite legal, notwithstanding.

One of the justices contradicted her, but she persisted. "It is false; for he only said that he had been at several meetings, both where was preaching the Word, and prayer, and that they had God's presence among them." Twisden replied angrily, "What, you think we can do what we list? Your husband is a breaker of the peace, and is convicted by the law." Hale called for the Statute Book. Elizabeth repeated, "My Lord, he was not lawfully convicted", but Chester contradicted her, crying, "It is recorded, woman, it is recorded." Elizabeth told of her interview with Lord Barkwood, and of his advice. "And now," she concluded, "I come to see if anything may be done in this business and you give me neither releasement nor relief." Twisden asked, "Will your husband leave preaching? If he will do so, then send for him." But Elizabeth knew the answer to that one. "My Lord, he dares not leave preaching, as long as he can speak." Twisden again said that John was a breaker of the peace, but Elizabeth replied that he desired to live peaceably, and to follow his calling and maintain his family; and, she added, "My Lord, I have four small children that cannot help themselves, of which one is blind, and have nothing to live upon but the charity of good people." Hale was touched. "Hast thou four children? Thou art but a young woman to have four children." "My Lord, I am but step-mother to them, having not been married to him yet full two years. Indeed, I was with child when my husband was first apprehended; but being young, and unaccustomed to such things, I being smayed at the news, fell into labour, and so continued for eight days, and then was delivered, but my child died." Hale was deeply touched, saying, "Alas, poor woman!"

But nothing came of it. The Statute Book was brought, but most probably the Judges took Paul Cobb's view of the matter. Sir Matthew Hale summed up the position. "I am sorry, woman, that I can do thee no good; thou must do one of three things, namely either to apply thyself to the king, or sue out his pardon, or get a writ of error. But a writ of error will be cheapest." So that was that. The last of three expedients meant applying to another Court to set aside Sir John Kelynge's ruling that John's statements were a confession of guilt, so that it might be condemned as bad law and the decision reversed and John freed. If John and his friends made any effort in this direction nothing came of it. John records Elizabeth's reaction to this last scene. "I remember that though I was somewhat timorous at my first entrance into the chamber, yet before I went out, I could not but break forth into tears, not so much because they were so hard-hearted against me and my husband, but to think what a sad account such poor creatures will have to give at the Coming of the Lord, when they shall there answer for all things whatsoever they have done in the body, whether it be good or whether it be bad."

9

By this it may be observed that she had the root of the matter in her. This attitude was a mark of the Puritan conscience also, which was so strong in her husband and those who thought as he did. The supreme concern in the hearts and minds of Puritans was a concern about God—to know him truly, serve him rightly, and thus glorify him. Conscience to them was that organ of the soul through which God brought his Word to bear on them. Nothing was more important to them than that a man's conscience should be enlightened, cleansed, and made sensitive to the will and ways of God. One recalls Martin Luther's momentous words at Worms, "My conscience is captive to the Word of God. I cannot and will not recant anything, for to go against conscience is neither right nor safe. God help me. Amen." Conscience to the Reformers and Puritans meant a man's knowledge of himself as standing in God's presence, subject to God's Word, and exposed to the judgements of God's law. So within their own society the Puritans were distinguished by their endeavour to please God at all times, at work, at home, in society, at recreation, in politics, in church matters—to examine their consciences daily and to discipline themselves by the standard of the Word of God. As a result they became sensitive to moral and political issues, and had great compassion for those in need. Years later John Bunyan was to give an account of conscience, as the Puritans understood it, in Mr Recorder of the town of Mansoul, in his *The Holy War*. "Mr Recorder was a man well read in the laws of his King, and also a man of courage and faithfulness, to speak truth at every occasion; and he had a tongue so bravely hung as he had a head filled with judgement." Conscience, to the Puritans, was a preacher to tell men of their duty towards God and towards man, and their concern to have a tender, enlightened conscience lent great ethical strength to their preaching.

John Bunyan next persuaded the gaoler to put his name down on the list of criminals awaiting trial at the March Assizes, and his friends approached the High Sheriff and the Judge, who promised that he would be called. But when the Assizes came on the Justices and Paul Cobb, Clerk of the Peace, removed his name. The latter was particularly angry, pointing out that John was not a prisoner awaiting trial, but one already tried and convicted.

It is not to be wondered at that, being kept in prison unjustly as he regarded it, and seeing effort after effort for his release come to nothing, he was sometimes very downcast, even at times beset by oppressive fears. Kelynge and Cobb, he reflected, had spoken of his being transported to Spain or Constantinople, "or even something worse", that is to say execution. Supposing this happened? Would he face it like a man or be fearful and trembling and bring dishonour on his faith? Such thoughts beset him quite often. And then, too, there was the plight of his family. "The parting with my wife and poor children hath often been to me in this place, as the pulling the flesh from my bones ... I often brought to mind the many hardships, miseries, and wants that my poor family was like to meet with, should I be taken from them, especially my poor blind child, who lay nearer my heart than all I had beside: O the thoughts of the hardship I thought my blind one might go under, would break my heart to pieces."

In order to support Elizabeth and the children, he set diligently to work in prison to make long-tagged thread-laces for riding boots and other footwear, and sold many hundreds gross of them to shop-keepers and other dealers. Elizabeth was busily engaged in pillow-lace making and in basket-making, which brought in some money. And John's friend, John Holden a Bedford brazier, also helped by using John's tools and equipment and taking on some of his regular work. This John Holden may well have been Elizabeth's brother, or some other relative of hers. Then there were the gifts of the wealthier members of the Bedford Meeting, and sometimes collections made on his behalf. It was a struggle, but their trust was in God and he supplied their need.

10

For the first months of John Bunyan's imprisonment he seems to have been given special favours from the gaoler, who on several occasions allowed him liberty to go beyond the prison walls. John even managed to preach in various places, in woods, isolated farmhouses, and fields. "I followed my wonted course of preaching, taking all occasions that were put into my hands to visit the people of God." He even got as far as London to see Christian friends there. In the earlier part of his imprisonment, he was also present at some of the meetings of the Church and took part in its affairs. On 28th August 1661, a Minute in the Church Book records "our brother Bunyan" was instructed to visit and remonstrate with two backsliders, brother Robert Nelson and Sister Manly. There were similar entries later on, and it is evident that brother Bunyan was highly regarded for his pastoral care and warnings. The Church was being harried, and had to meet in secret from place to place, sometimes as far afield as Haines or Gamlingay. The Church Book was locked away from 1664 to 1668 for safety's sake and no minutes were recorded. But prayer was made unceasingly by the elders and members for one another and the spiritual life of the Church was maintained bright and strong.

The new Restoration Parliament which met on the 8th May 1661 was almost entirely Tory and Anglican, and it proceeded to impose an Anglican pattern on the nation by means of four great penal laws known as the *Clarendon Code*, instigated by Edward Hyde, Earl of Clarendon, Charle's chief minister of state. The first was the Corporation Act, December 1661, which limited membership of municipal bodies to those who received Communion according to the rites of the Church of England. The second was the Act of Uniformity, which Kelynge drew up, which made the use of the Revised Prayer Book, 1662 and ordination by a bishop, compulsory for all ministers of religion. It was passed by the Commons by only 186 voted to 180, but its effect was to eject 2000 of the best clergy out of their livings, and to sever the connection between the Church of England and other Protestant bodies on the Continent. The King did not care for it, because he had strong Catholic preferences, and hoped to bring in toleration for Romanists by granting toleration for Nonconformists.

In May 1664 a new Conventicle Act was passed, forbidding all religious meetings except those of the Established Church. The fourth of Clarendon's acts was the Five Mile Act of October 1665, passed at Oxford where Parliament was sitting owing to the plague in London. This act forbade Nonconformists ministers to teach in schools or to live within five miles of a corporate town. This resulted in hundreds of faithful Puritan preachers and teachers being deprived of their work and banished to obscure places.

This repressive legislation caused great dismay and trial to thousands of people. They had grown to love the simplicity of Dissenting worship, extempore prayer, plain exposition of Scripture and the right to choose their own pastors outside the ranks of those ordained by bishops. But they determined to suffer for their convictions, and to make a stand for liberty of worship. Britain and the United States of America owe much to their faithfulness and fortitude.

11

To a man of vigorous spirit, like John Bunyan, used to an active outdoor occupation, it was a grievous thing to be confined to prison. But he had much to occupy him. Besides making the tag-laces, he spent much time in reading and writing. At first he had only two books, the Bible and Foxe's *Book of Martyrs* (a fitting companion for a man in his situation). His copy published in 1641 had his name in large capitals, John Bunyan, at the foot of the title page, and the date 1662. It is to be seen in the Bedford Library. As to his writing, in the first six years of his imprisonment he wrote no fewer than nine of the books which presented the Christian Faith to thousands of poor Christians throughout the country. He reached more by his pen than ever he could have done by his voice. As the months passed by and persecution of Nonconformists increased, the County Gaol became crowded with ministers and laymen, even including a few women. They held daily meetings for prayer and Bible study. A visitor wrote, "I have heard Mr Bunyan both preach and pray with that mighty spirit of faith, and plerophry of divine assistance, that has made me stand and wonder."

There was a well-known story of Bunyan in his early prison days, that on one occasion, when the gaoler gave him liberty to go out, he was seized with a spirit of misgiving, and came back before he was expected. He had not returned long before one of the magistrates came to enquire if all the prisoners were in, and especially if John Bunyan was safe. The gaoler, immensely relieved at being able to produce John for inspection, told him he might go out when he liked, for he surely knew better than the gaoler when to return. News of John's ventures abroad, however, were soon known to the authorities, and the gaoler was threatened with dire punishment if they continued. Other gaolers came and went through Bunyan's twelve years in prison, some kind and others harsh. But there was no more preaching outside.

12

In his book *The Life and Death of Mr Badman*, published in 1680, he says, "When I was in prison there came a woman to me that was under a great deal of trouble." It turned out that she was in service to a shopkeeper at Wellingborough, whose till she had robbed again and again. Smitten with remorse she came to ask Bunyan what she should do, being moved to do so by having read one or other of his books. He pointed her to the One who forgives repentant sinners, and counselled her to make restitution to her master. Though in prison he was the spiritual guide of some who were outside.

Some of the stalwarts of the Bedford Church soon joined him in prison, Samuel and John Fenn and many more. John Donne the ejected Rector of Pertenhall in the north of the county, sentenced to banishment before 1668 was still in Bedford Gaol in 1672. William Wheeler, ejected from Cranfield, and John Wright the pious saddler of Blunham, were also there and many more of John's Puritan friends. On one occasion sixty of them meeting in a wood, were surprised by the officers of the law and the whole company marched off to prison. The whole gaol became a conventicle! The overcrowding must have been very uncomfortable, but though John Bunyan could not go out to a congregation, a congregation was brought to him! The day room on the first floor which John Howard the prison reformer tells us was used as a chapel surely witnessed stirring scenes. Some of the sermons John delivered there were afterwards turned into books, such as the *Holy City*, published in 1665.

In this atmosphere and situation John Bunyan made rapid strides to full maturity in spiritual things, culminating in his writing his autobiography, *Grace Abounding to the Chief of Sinners*, published in 1666. "I have continued in this condition (i.e. in prison) with much content through grace." He had indeed. And in his valuable book, *Christian*

Behaviour (1663), he writes, "When Christians stand every one in their places and do the work of their relations (i.e. work that relates to them), then they are like the flowers in the garden, that stand and grow where the gardener hath planted them, and then they shall both honour the garden in which they are planted and the gardener that hath so disposed of them. From the hyssop on the wall to the cedar in Lebanon, their fruit is their glory." There was calm amidst the stress and strain. There was no bitterness of spirit on account of his treatment, for in his heart grace reigned.

There were lighter moments also. Years before while still at Elstow, he had made a violin, after an Italian pattern, of thin iron plates on his brazier's anvil, inscribing on it his name "John Bunyan, Helstow", with a graving tool. Now, in prison, he spent many secret hours in shaping a flute from the rail of his prison stool. He carefully hollowed the wood and used his candle flame to burn the small note-holes in the barrel. When finished, the flute gave forth faint musical notes, and in the evenings, after the gaoler had made his rounds, he played on it with zest, hurriedly replacing it in the stool when the gaoler, surprised by the sound, returned to find its source. He never did. John little dreamed that centuries afterwards both violin and flute would be rediscovered and preserved as hallowed relics of his life. They are to be seen in the Bunyan Meeting, Bedford.

The months of his imprisonment lengthened into years and his children were growing up. Blind Mary, already in her teens, knew how to find her way to the County Gaol with food or mugs of soup, and always with devoted love. Elizabeth was growing tall, John and Thomas were becoming sturdy little boys and their father made alphabetical bricks for them. Wife Elizabeth came constantly to visit him, to tell him of the family, and comfort his heart.

13

Soon after the publication of *Grace Abounding* in 1666 he enjoyed a few brief weeks of release from prison. The unknown writer of the continuation of this book in 1692 says that after six years of confinement "by the intercession of some in trust and power, that took pity upon his suffering, he obtained his freedom." We have no idea who these friends were. It is possible that Sir Matthew Hale had a hand in it, or some influential London Nonconformists. At all events he went home to the house in St Cuthbert's parish, reunited with his wife and family.

In 1665 the Great Plague swept London and far beyond, one of many periodic visitations which had terrified England since the Black Death. The awful cry, "Bring out your dead," sounded through London. The Court moved to Oxford. Many Nonconformist ministers banished from London by the Five Mile Act returned to the capital to minister to the sick and dying. In one week in September the Lord Mayor of London recorded that 7,165 persons had died of the plague. The pestilence reached Bedford in 1666, and no fewer than forty persons died of it north of the river. Things were far worse in Newport Pagnell where 697 people were buried, including John's old friend the bookseller, Matthias Cowley. That same year saw the death, though not by plague, of Christopher Hall, Vicar of Elstow, whose sermon against Sunday sports had begun the process that led to John's conversion.

Early in September 1666 the Great Fire of London occurred, which destroyed old St Paul's and the heart of the city, including shops, warehouses, private dwellings and 88 city churches. Samuel Pepys gathered up his money and plate and moved them into the country, as did many more. "The saddest sight of desolation I ever saw," he wrote in his diary. The fire affected John Bunyan, though he did not realise it at the time, because the sheets of the first printing of *Grace Abounding* were destroyed by it. A contemporary writer says that "the late dreadful Fire proved extremely prejudicial and destructive to most Companies in the City, yet none of them received so grand losses and damage by the devouring Conflagration as the Company of Stationers, most of whose habitations, store-houses, shops, together with all their stocks, books, bound and unbound (by reason of their combustableness and difficulty to remove them) were not only consumed in a moment, but their ashes and scorched leaves were scattered in sundry places above 16 miles from the City." The first edition of *Grace Abounding* is thus exceedingly rare, and the British Museum Library did not obtain its sole copy until 1883. The book itself, however, made John Bunyan's name widely known, and brought inspiration and comfort to countless hundreds in those dark days.

Free for a few weeks John Bunyan resumed preaching and visiting his friends. Charles Doe, a later friend and hero-worshipper of John, tells us that "a little after his release they took him again at a meeting, and put him in the same gaol, where he lay six years more." Where this arrest was made we do not know, but it was most probably in some field or wood thought to be safe from observation. A strong tradition exists that the subject he was to preach upon was, "Dost thou believe in the Son of God?", and that he had given out his text when the constable appeared—who turned pale and let go of Bunyan's arm, whereupon John exclaimed, "See how this man trembles at the Word of God!" Trembling or not the constable speedily conveyed him to Bedford Gaol, there to spend six more long years.

Of this second period in prison we know very little. No doubt the routine was much the same, with constant prayer meetings and sermons for the prisoners. It is curious, however, that he produced only two books during this time, his *Confession of Faith*, and *A Defence of the Doctrine of Justification by Faith*. This comparative silence is surprising, but the explanation may well be that his London publisher friend, Francis Smith, was out of favour with the authorities, and could not get his books licensed. Or could it be that John's mind and pen were now busy upon his greatest work?

8

Pastor of the Flock

1

In April 1671 Charles II prorogued Parliament, which was not called together for two years, and unchecked by the Commons did much as he liked. National affairs were in a bad way. Clarendon had been dismissed and Charles passed from policy to policy as easily as from mistress to mistress. Always there was the need for more and more money, which Charles spent before it was raised. He was in debt to the City and to many private merchants. The Dutch War had been disastrous for England; de Ruyter sailed up the Medway and burnt unopposed the shipping in Chatham docks. John Evelyn beheld the enemy fleet lying unchallenged and at ease at the mouth of the Thames, "as dreadful a spectacle as ever an Englishman saw." "People make nothing of talking treason in the streets openly," recorded Samuel Pepys, "and everybody nowadays reflects upon Oliver and commends him." But although Oliver had passed from the scene there were many thousands throughout the land of the same staunch Puritan principles and steadfast faith.

Charles entered into still closer relations with France which made him practically the pensioner of the French King, Louis XIV. In 1670 he signed the secret Treaty of Dover which pledged Charles to acknowledge himself a Roman Catholic and to bring Britain back under the Popish sway. In return he received from Louis a pension of £200,000 per annum (an immense sum in the values of the day), and the promise of troops if he was resisted by Protestants. This policy met with considerable opposition, but Charles controlled the first standing army England had ever had. The King was indolent and extravagant, and his Court was a hotbed of immorality, gaming, and intrigue, yet somehow he managed to be a popular monarch. And he could be a shrewd politician when it suited him. In order to carry out this French policy he made the first move in issuing a *Declaration of Indulgence* in March 1672, with the aim of changing the Government's official religious policy in order to benefit Roman Catholics as well as Nonconformists.

2

The king was jogged into this action, so to speak, by one of his humble subjects, whom almost all Bunyan's biographers have overlooked, and who was largely responsible for his release from prison, and that of thousands of others. Not long before, at his morning levée, Charles had noticed a stranger whose face was vaguely familiar. He prided himself on never forgetting faces, and searched his memory for a clue as to who this could be. And then he realised ... Gone in a moment was the elegant palace of Whitehall in which he lounged, and his mind reverted to the terrible and dangerous days after the Battle of Worcester, in hiding, and seeking escape overseas. He saw again Shoreham Creek in the twilight, heard the sound of the waves on the shingle, the forlorn cry of the sea-birds, felt the wind on his face; felt, once again, the strong arms of a swarthy fisherman as he was carried out to a boat a little off shore. Yes, it all came back as in a remembered dream. He stared across the crowded room —it was the same man who had carried him to the boat and tended him in the tiny cabin, Richard Carver. He summoned the man to his side, wrung his hand and thanked him once again for helping him to escape to France. He had been the mate of Tattersall's fishing boat that night long ago and he had come, he said, for his reward. Charles' brow darkened just a little. Reward? Was everyone he met self-seeking? But Carver did not demand money. He had been converted, he told the king, and was now a Quaker. Since there were 8,000 Quakers in prison, would Charles not exercise his prerogative of mercy and release them? In eloquent words he pleaded for their release, and Charles, much moved, gave a kindly answer.

Since it suited his policy well, the Declaration of Indulgence was issued, and mercy extended not only to Quakers but to all other Nonconformists as well. He was too cunning to announce his adherence to Romanism, but indulgence to Dissenters—by all means. The king's Declaration admitted that "it was evident by the sad experience of twelve years that there is very little fruit of all these forcible courses", i.e. the repressive legislation of the Clarendon Code. It continued, "That there be no pretence for any of Our Subjects to continue their illegal meetings and conventicles, We do Declare, That we shall from time to time allow a sufficient number of places, as they shall be desired, in all parts of this Our Kingdom, for the use of such as do not conform to the Church of England, to meet and assemble in, in order to their Public Worship and Devotion; which places shall be open and free to all persons." Nonconformist meeting-houses were to be licensed by the Secretary of State upon application from the Minister, and more than 3,000 licenses were applied for. Thus after twelve years Charles did something about those of "tender conscience" he had promised to help when he landed in England, and Richard Carver, the fisherman of Sussex, played a vital part in it. Let him not be forgotten!

3

The prison doors opened, and thousands of England's finest citizens, including John Bunyan, stepped out into freedom again after their long ordeal. John, when first arrested, had been a broad-shouldered young man of robust health, from perpetually tramping and riding in the open air. Twelve years later, although only forty-three, there were many grey hairs in his auburn hair, many lines on his forehead, and a paleness on his cheeks. His memory, too, was scarred with the impact of what he had seen and felt, the stench of the rat-infested dungeon, the bitter cold of winter, the quarrels among the felons, the vicious practices of long-term criminals, the cruelty and corruption of some of the gaolers, the deaths among his fellow believers. Yet, he had his happy memories also: the joy of Christian fellowship, the blessedness of the prayer-meetings, the inspiration of the preaching, and above all his visions of Heaven and the road to it. There was also, for John was very human, the astonishing fact that he had become an author, and had been enabled to use his pen for the service of God and the furtherance of the Gospel.

After twelve years in prison, and since the publication of *Grace Abounding*, and his other works, Bunyan's status had markedly changed, and he was recognised as a wise and reliable leader of the Nonconformists. The Bedford Church, after prolonged meetings and much prayer, solemnly appointed John to be their Pastor on 21st January 1672. The Church Book recording this adds, "And he accepting thereof, gave up himself to serve Christ and His Church in that charge; and received of the Elders the right hand of fellowship." Seven of the most reliable members were appointed deacons to assist him in the pastorate, some of whom had been in prison with him—John Fenn, Oliver Scott, Luke Astwood, Thomas Cooper, Edward Dent, Edward Isaac, and Nehemiah Cox. In spite of all the repressive measures Nonconformity was everywhere on the increase. In Bedford itself the 30 Nonconformists of 1669 had grown to 121 in 1676, according to a religious census ordered by Archbishop Sheldon. In the whole county there were about 1000; the Quakers numbered 390, the Anabaptists 277, and the Independents 220.

John Bunyan lost no time in applying for a license for a place of worship, not only for the Bedford Meeting, but also for other small congregations associated with it in various villages, whom also he was to shepherd. In May 1672 he applied for his own license to preach, and also for twenty-five other teachers, and for thirty buildings, mostly houses and barns, as meeting places. The Bedford Independents had acquired an orchard and barn which belonged to Josias Ruffhead. It was conveyed to "John Bunyan, of the Towne of Bedford, brasier", and to five of his colleagues, for £50, "to be a place for the use of such as do not conforme to the Church of England, who are of the persuasion commonly called Congregational". It stood in Mill Street, quite near John's own home in St Cuthbert's Street. The barn was commodious, and when cleaned and fitted with forms and a pulpit made a fine meeting place. On the same site now stands the Bunyan Meeting.

His license dated 9th May, 1672 was for him "to teach as a Congregational Person"—not, be it noted, as a Baptist. It had to be shown to the civil authorities when he was away from home, as it was at Leicester in October, when he preached in a house close to St Nicholas Church, and showed his precious license to "Mr Mayor, Mr Overing, Mr Freeman, and Mr Browne", who duly chronicled his visit in the Borough Records.

4

But his office as Pastor of the Bedford Church and its associate congregations, kept him mostly in his own county for a while. He was soon busy preaching in Bedford, Haines, Ridgmont, Steventon, Pavenham, Kempston and many other villages. Indeed, so active was he that he was called "Bishop Bunyan" by some, a term he would have much disliked. Many of the Congregational and Baptist Churches over a wide area are said to have been formed through his preaching. He was now mature in his Christian experience, and his preaching was more balanced, although not less scriptural than formerly. Sometimes he went further afield to preach at Hitchin, Luton, Cambridge, Reading and London. He had many Nonconformist connections with London and usually preached there two or three times a year. Charles II heard that Dr John Owen greatly admired Bunyan's preaching, and asked in surprise how a learned man such as he could sit and listen to an illiterate tinker. Said Owen, "May it please your Majesty, I would gladly give up all my learning for that tinker's power of preaching". Owen often heard Bunyan preach in London.

In *The Pilgrim's Progress* the Interpreter takes Christian into his house and shows him a picture hanging on the wall. It was the picture of a "very grave person"—it had "eyes lift up to Heaven, the best of Books in his hand, the Law of Truth was written upon his lips, the World was behind his back; it stood as if it pleaded with men, and a Crown of Gold did hang over his head." It is a portrait of the Gospel preacher, such as John Bunyan was himself, and it is a challenging example to all Christian preachers of every age.

Being Pastor of the Bedford Church meant not only preaching but visitation, personal exhortation, and pastoral discipline. The Church Book gives many instances of this latter duty. Edward Dent of Gamlingay was dismissed for mismanaging his sister's affairs. John noted in 1678 that he had to admonish Mary Fosket for scandalmongering against Bro. Honylove. In February 1679 John Stanton was reproved for beating his wife. Other entries refer to members being lax in attendance at worship, or "walking disorderly" in the ways of the world. John maintained with the utmost constancy the principles on which the Church had been founded by John Gifford, with a wise tolerance on matters not fundamental to the Faith. Nevertheless, new members were received only after careful examination of their spiritual state, and neither Arminians nor those guilty of dishonesty, gambling, or Sabbath-breaking were accepted.

The Pastor had trouble with a man named John Wildman, who in 1680 at a church meeting made charges against the congregation "with very great passion", and also accused

John of scandalous financial misbehaviour. The Church listened gravely and then pronounced him "an abominable liar and slanderer". He was eventually cast out. It is likely that his portrait is partly drawn in "Mr Badman".

John Bunyan had a true pastoral heart. "If any of those who were awakened by my Ministry did fall back", he tells us, "as sometimes too many did, I can truly say their loss hath been more to me than if one of my own children, begotten of my body, had been going to the grave ... I have counted as if I had goodly buildings and lordships in those places where my children (i.e. converts) were born; my heart hath been so wrapped up in the glory of this excellent work, that I counted myself more blessed and honoured by God by this than if He had made me the Emperor of the Christian World, or the Lord of all the glory of the earth without it." And although he wrote this about his early preaching it would surely be even more true of his fuller pastoral responsibility. He would be prayerful and faithful also, in visiting the sick and the dying.

John's family now consisted of Mary, Elizabeth, John and Thomas by his first wife, Mary; and Sarah and Joseph by his second wife, Elizabeth. It is interesting to note that Sarah and Joseph were baptized in St Cuthbert's Church and that Elizabeth his wife, like Mary before her, was not a member of Bunyan's Church. It would seem that she preferred Anglican worship. His father, Thomas Bunyan, now in his seventieth year, still lived at Bedford, and surely not without pride in his son in spite of all. John's own brother, Thomas, was received into fellowship with the Bedford Church in 1673.

Bunyan's earliest Christian impressions and knowledge had come to him through the services in the Abbey Church, Elstow, where the Prayer Book of Edward VI was in use, at least in part. Although he later resisted all efforts to make him accept and conform to the Prayer Book, he was still influenced by the order and reverence of the liturgical worship. The Revised Prayer Book of 1662 he probably saw later, and it was undoubtedly enriched with new prayers and services. But for himself he much preferred extempore prayer, inspired by the Spirit at the time of its use. Some years before his death he roundly condemned that loose and slovenly kind of public prayer that often degraded "free worship" in his day, and also in our own. "It is at this day wonderful common," he declared in *The Pharisee and the Publican*, "for men to pray extempore. He is counted nobody, now, that cannot at any moment, at a minute's warning, make a prayer of half-an-hour long." He is not against extempore prayer, he says, "for I believe it is the best kind of praying, but there are a great many such prayers made, especially in pulpits and public meetings that are without the Holy Ghost and therefore unedifying. Wit and reason and notion are now screwed up to a very great height; nor do men want words and fancies or pride to make them do this thing."

Of his preaching he tells us in *Grace Abounding*, "In my preaching I have really been in pain, and have as it were travailled to bring forth children to God; neither could I be satisfied unless some fruits did appear in my work. If I were fruitless, it mattered not who commended me; but if I were fruitful, I cared not who did condemn. It pleased me nothing to see some people drink in opinions if they seemed ignorant of Jesus Christ, and the worth of their own salvation, sound conviction of sin, especially for unbelief, and an heart set on fire to be saved by Christ, with strong breathings after a truly sanctified soul. That it was that delighted me; these were the souls I counted blessed."

5

He was not much impressed with those in the Church that seemed to have great gifts, but were really like lifeless, clanging cymbals. "A little love, a little grace, a little of the true fear of God, is better than all these gifts ... Let all men prize a little with the fear of the Lord. Gifts indeed are desirable, but yet Great Grace and small Gifts are better than great Gifts and no Grace."

Satan, so he asserted, designed to overthrow his ministry.

Rumours were spread about him that he was a witch, a Jesuit, a highwayman even. Others claimed with the boldest confidence "that I had my Misses, my whores, my bastards, yea two wives at once, and the like". "To all which I shall only say, God knows that I am innocent ... My foes have missed the mark in their shooting at me. I am not the man. I wish that they themselves be guiltless. If all the fornicators and adulterers were hanged by the neck till they be dead, John Bunyan, the object of their envy, would still be alive and well."

More serious than these slanders, however, was the case of Agnes Beaumont in 1674. From 1670 the Bedford Church occasionally held its meetings at Gamlingay, fifteen miles away on the Cambridgeshire border. The meetings were held in a barn, and here one day John met Agnes Beaumont from the village of Edworth. She was twenty, and on her conversion had been received into the Bedford Church by Bunyan. She was a lively country lass and evidently much drawn to her Pastor. She lived with her widowed father, John Beaumont, in a farmhouse at Edworth. Her brother and his wife, although not members of the Church, were Puritans, and often attended John's preaching. Originally her father also had held Nonconformist views, but a malicious neighbour poisoned his mind against both the Bedford Meeting and Bunyan himself.

In February 1674 Agnes, with difficulty, obtained her father's permission to go to Gamlingay for a meeting. But how should she get there, for mud and thawing snow made the seven-mile walk impossible? The only available horse was to be used by her brother taking his wife on the pillion. So it was arranged that John Wilson, who was travelling from Hitchin, should call and take her pillion-wise. When the day came Wilson did not appear. Instead, quite unexpectedly, John Bunyan rode up, and called at her brother's home. They urged him to take Agnes to the meeting and, very reluctantly, he agreed. So Agnes mounted the horse behind John and off they started. Unfortunately her father saw them from a field and was very angry. More than this, they were recognised as they rode into Gamlingay by a clergyman named Lane, a man who hated all Nonconformists.

The meeting over, John Bunyan told Agnes that he must return to Bedford by another route, and entrusted her to the care of another woman who walked with her most of the way home through the mud. Arriving at the farm she found the door bolted against her, and her father, furious with her, shouted out of the window that he would not let her in unless she promised to give up attending the Bedford Church meetings. She would not promise. So, tired, wet and miserable, Agnes spent a frosty night in the barn, and then went to stay with her brother for a few days. A night or so later, John Beaumont was seized with a fatal illness and died before morning.

When Lane heard of this he began to spread disreputable stories at Baldock where he lived, which soon spread to other places. Agnes had been wooed by a Mr Farrow, a lawyer, whose suit she had rejected. There appeared to be every probability that he had hoped, by marrying Agnes, to inherit all or some of her father's property. He now saw an opportunity to get his revenge, and started a rumour that Agnes had obtained poison from John Bunyan, a widower, so that she might be free to marry him. Bunyan, of course, was not a widower, and only the most credulous or vindictive would have given credence to such a tale. But many did. These dramatic and titillating tales caused a stir in Edworth and district. The coroner was called in, and it was proved beyond doubt that Beaumont had died from natural causes. So Agnes' innocence was established, and the malicious accusers confounded. Agnes lived to marry two husbands, and to survive John Bunyan by more than thirty years. She also lived to write the story, *The Narrative of the Persecution of Agnes Beaumont in 1674*. She died in 1720 and is buried in the graveyard of Tilehouse Street Chapel, Hitchin, where a wall tablet commemorates her story. It must have been a trying time for John Bunyan but trust in his Lord carried him through.

6

Early in February 1675 Charles II once again changed his policy, under pressure from the re-called House of Commons. They demanded the recall of the Declaration of Indulgence; if not, no money would be granted. Charles gave way, and calling for the Declaration solemnly broke the seal with his own hands. The licenses issued under the Indulgence were declared null and void, and another period of persecution for Dissenters began. One of the first to feel the effect was John Bunyan. He received a secret warning of impending arrest. On the 4th March 1675 a warrant for his arrest, signed by thirteen county magistrates was issued, for repeatedly preaching at a conventicle during the previous month. The penalty fixed by the Conventicle Act of 1670 was not prison but a fine of £20 for a first offence, and £40 thereafter. If the fine were not paid his goods and chattels could be taken. By no means could John pay such a fine, and so for eighteen months he went "underground", and was on the run. The warrant is now in a New York library. Many hundreds of Nonconformists had their goods seized in lieu of payment of fines.

Once again John was dependent on the help of such friends as John Wilson of Hitchin, the Foster Brothers of Hunsden House and many others. But he was still active in the service of the Gospel although most careful to avoid arrest. Meetings were held at night, in remote places or in the woods. More than once he had to hide in a chimney or cupboard, or make a hurried exit from a back-door into the woods. Near Hunsden House was Wainwood Dell, a natural amphitheatre surrounded by trees, and here in the depth of night worshippers would steal in from the surrounding countryside to hear John expound the Scriptures. It was like old times! Sometimes he went to Hitchin or Luton. On one occasion, disguised as a drover, whip in hand, he went to Reading and preached.

The warrant had to be served personally, so there was no alternative but for John to leave Bedford and stay hidden in the homes of friends, who gave him loyal and practical support.

Foiled in their attempt to lay hands on John Bunyan by means of the warrant, the authorities tried another procedure.Two or three years earlier he had been accused by the Vicar and church-wardens of St Cuthbert's for refusing to come to Church and receive the Sacrament, whereupon he was excommunicated by Dr Fuller, bishop of Lincoln in which diocese Bedford then was. John, summoned to appear before the Archdeacon, did not appear, and the sentence was passed in his absence.

Eighteen months after the issue of the abortive warrant in March 1675, John was arrested by the Sheriff under the older legal machinery of non-attendance at church. No details are available of the arrest, but he was back again in Bedford County Gaol for a further short period. In the diocesan archives at Lincoln are details of the Visitation of the Archdeaconry of Bedford in 1674, where it is reported that "John Bunnion, tincker" of the town of Bedford stood excommunicated for refusing to come to church and receive the sacrament. A man taken on a writ of "de excommunicato capiendo" was the king's prisoner, and it is difficult to resist the conclusion that the Sheriff would commit Bunyan to the County Gaol, not the tiny lock-up on the bridge, even if it was still standing, which is doubtful.

Now there was a law that if any two persons would go to the Bishop of the diocese and offer a cautionary bond that the prisoner should conform in half a year, the bishop might release him upon that bond. This stratagem on John's behalf was attempted and it succeeded. This bond, discovered in Aylesbury Museum in 1887, is dated the 21st June, 1677. The sureties who undertook that John should conform within six months were two London Nonconformists, friends made in his London preaching visits, Thomas Kelsey and Robert Blaney. They knew perfectly well that he would not conform, but they probably expected that once he was released nothing more would happen. In London his good friend Dr John Owen approached the Bishop of Lincoln, now Dr Thomas

Barlow, on his behalf. Such was Dr Owen's influence and reputation that this would have been a weighty recommendation. So the bond was accepted and he was released, and nothing further was heard of his accusation.

His perilous freedom ended, to the relief of Elizabeth Bunyan, John was back home once more, and ready to resume the pages of *The Pilgrim's Progress*.

9

The Pilgrim's Progress

Lord Macaulay has left on record his assessment of the work which was to make John Bunyan's name famous through-out the world. "We are not afraid to say, that though there were many clever men in England during the latter half of the seventeenth century, there were only two great creative minds. One of those produced the *Paradise Lost*, and the other *The Pilgrim's Progress*." John had no idea that he was producing a masterpiece. He could not guess what place his allegory would have in English literature. His over-riding concern was to use fiction in order to make truth clear and goodness attractive. Rudyard Kipling in a well-known poem describes him as

> The Father of the novel,
> Salvation's first Defoe.

And Vera Brittain remarks that salvation is as fit a subject for a novel as any other theme.

1

Part One of *The Pilgrim's Progress* was first published in 1678. But when was it written and where? Since the bond for his release from his second imprisonment is dated 21st June

1677 he could not have been in prison before the autumn of 1676, and as it is clear that he was in the County Gaol for only a comparatively short period he was probably released sometime in 1677, very likely the 21st June. As we have already shown the long-held tradition that the book was written in the town lock-up on Bedford Bridge can no longer be sustained.

John Bunyan himself tells us that his allegory was a prison book. It begins thus: "As I walked through the wilderness of this world I lighted upon a certain place where was a Den, and I laid me down in that place to sleep; and as I slept I dreamed a dream." In the third edition, which was the first *complete* edition, for he had added many incidents and characters to the story, he wrote in the margin against this sentence—"The Gaol." In his rhymed "Author's Apology for his Book" he says that the idea came to him while engaged on another work.

> I writing of the way
> And race of saints in this our Gospel day,
> Fell suddenly into an Allegory ...

What was this other book? Dr John Brown basing his assumption on the theory that John Bunyan was put into the Bridge prison in 1675 thinks the book was *The Strait Gate* published in 1676. But it does not fit John's description. There is one book, however, that does, written during his long first imprisonment, called *"A Confession of my Faith; and a Reason for my Practice, or with whom and who not, I can hold Church Fellowship*. It was published in 1672.

It has puzzled most biographers of Bunyan why, seeing he was such a prolific author in the first part of his imprisonment, issuing nine books between 1660 and 1666, there should be a gap of six years before *A Confession of my Faith* in 1672. This silence is accounted for if he was engaged in beginning *The Pilgrim's Progress*. As he wrote the *Confession of my Faith* it suddenly struck him how effective it would be to set forth the Christian's pathway to Heaven, and the truths associated with it, in fictional or allegorical form. He remembered his youthful delight in stories such as *Bevis of Southampton, George on Horseback, The Seven Champions of Christendom*. What if he could set out the Christian life and trials and triumphs in story form? *The Pilgrim's Progress* ...! Yes, that was it exactly. His own spiritual experiences, and the folk he had met on his journey to Heaven, would supply much material. And his vigorous imagination, made true and faithful by his constant reading of the Bible, would add much to it. So he began, jotting down scraps from time to time over the years between 1666 when *Grace Abounding* was published, and 1672 when *A Confession of my Faith* saw the light. On his release from prison in 1672 Part One was unfinished, and his busy preaching and oversight of the Bedford Church and associated congregations from 1672 to 1676 when he was again arrested, left him no time to complete the book. But, on finding himself in the County Gaol in Silver Street again, he set to work once more with renewed zest to complete the great Allegory. This seems to be the true way to account for the circumstances of the writing of *The Pilgrim's Progress, Part One*. He pondered many years before writing his Autobiography, *Grace Abounding*. It seems certain that long contemplation preceded the writing of his classic work.

There is a puzzling break in the story after Christian and Hopeful leave the shepherds in the Delectable Mountains. "So I awoke from my Dream." Many writers have taken this to indicate that at this point he was released from his second imprisonment and finished the story at home. But it can equally mean that he had reached this point when his *first* imprisonment ended, that he was unable to continue it during the three or four years of pastoral activity, and that he returned to it and finished Part One during his second imprisonment. This second stay in prison ended in June 1677. Part One of *The Pilgrim's Progress* was entered at Stationers' Hall on the 22nd December 1677, and licensed for publication on the 18th February 1678.

2

Bunyan wrote his great book for Puritans of the lower and middle classes, and religious books were almost their only reading. The idea that life is a pilgrimage through this world to the next was not a new one. Sir Walter Raleigh was only one to give expression to this, as in his poem, "His Pilgrimage". In the Middle Ages the great roads were crowded with pilgrims going to hallowed shrines. Many Bible passages spoke of the journey of life, the way to Heaven. It is John Bunyan's achievement that he wrote in simple style, but with consummate power, the story of such a pilgrimage so that the story never dulls, and the narrative sweeps on to its conclusion with the force of genius.

We first meet Christian with a Book in his hand, and a great burden on his back. It is the Book, the revealed Word of God, that has made him conscious of his burden and the awful consequences if he is not delivered from the guilt and power of his sin. While still in the City of Destruction he longs for peace with God, deliverance from the burden, and to set out on the road to Heaven. The Book he is reading makes him cry out, "What must I do to be saved?" It is then that Evangelist draws near and sets him upon the right road. So, turning his back on the City of Destruction he starts out, and presently comes to the Cross where his burden tumbles away from him. Every Puritan reader would, from his own experience, understand and appreciate the significance of such an opening, and would identify with the varying situations and trials through which Christian had to go before he reached at length the Celestial City.

One cause of the success of *The Pilgrim's Progress* was its style. It spoke to the unlettered reader in words he could understand. His speech was the speech of the Bible, and knowing the Bible well the Puritans could follow his arguments. But if Bunyan is plàin he is never vulgar; although full of metaphor he is not obscure, going straight to the point in the fewest words. Lord Macaulay recommends Bunyan's style as "an invaluable study to every person who wishes to gain a wide command over the English language. Its vocabulary is the vocabulary of the common people. There is not an expression, if we except a few technical terms of theology, that would puzzle the rudest peasant. "He goes on to point out that there are whole pages which do not contain a single word of more than two syllables. "Its English," says J.R. Green, "is the simplest and homeliest English that has ever been used by any great English writer, but it is the English of the Bible."

The secret of its unique position in literature is its human interest and dramatic power. The people John wrote about were real people, with real problems and weaknesses. Christian, the Pilgrim, is John Bunyan himself, as he knew himself to be within his own soul; and his experiences, spiritual and otherwise, are those which he himself had experienced, and set down in *Grace Abounding*.

The characters we meet with on the road, each one distinct with his or her own individual traits of manner and language, are those Bunyan had seen and known. Some he had met in his soldiering days, some in the ale-house, some at the fairs on Elstow Green, some in the Bedford Meeting. But they were, every one, true to life. Dean Stanley aptly comments, "We, as well as he, have met with Mr Bye-ends, and Mr Facing-both-ways, and Mr Talkative. Some of us, perhaps, have seen Mr No-good and Mr Live-loose, Mr Hatelight, and Mr Implacable. All of us have at times been like Mr Ready-to-halt, Mr Feeblemind, and Faintheart, Noheart, and Slowpace, Shortwind, and the young woman whose name was Dull." Yes, indeed we have. And we have also sometimes been in the Slough of Despond, Doubting Castle, and on the Delectable Mountains. Bunyan's intimate knowledge of human nature and human life in their everyday guise, gave him great power to hold our attention and to charm as well as to instruct.

Many writers have been at pains to make such places as the Interpreter's House, the House Beautiful, Doubting Castle, and the Delectable Mountains—even the place somewhat ascending—represent places, mansions and scenery around

Bedford that John knew well. Such efforts at identification are vain and unnecessary; these places are drawn from his imagination as much as from his observation. And so are his happily-chosen place-names, with a shrewd underlying truth to them all—"Temporary, who dwelt in Graceless, two miles off from Honesty, next door to one Turnback"; or "Talkative, the son of one Saywell, who dwelt in Prating Row"; or "Beelzebub's friend, Sir Having Greedy", and "Turnaway, that dwelt in the town of Apostacy"; or "Valiant-for-the Truth, born in Darkland, where his father and mother still were". Gwilym O. Griffith remarks, "Not Dickens himself, within a like compass, will give us a richer gallery of living, unforgettable types."

3

It has often been pointed out that there are some imperfections in *The Pilgrim's Progress*. What book is without them? And given the circumstances of the book's writing, the wonder is that there are not more. But some there undoubtedly are. How was it that Faithful was carried up to the Heavenly City in the middle of the pilgrimage without crossing the River of Death? Why did Hopeful join Christian along the road having never passed through the Wicket-Gate or lost his burden at the foot of the Cross? And in Part Two, the Wicket Gate has become a considerable building with a summer parlour, while the shepherds' tents on the Delectable Mountains have given place to a Palace with a dining room and store of jewels. The Town of Vanity, also, has greatly changed in Part Two, and Christiana and her family settle down there comfortably and enjoy the society of the place, while her sons marry and have children. Bunyan must have overlooked the character of the place he described in Part One when he wrote Part Two. And what about Christiana's "sweet babes" who are terrified of the dog at the Wicket Gate, and cry at having to climb the hill, and whose faces are stroked by the Interpreter, who sup on bread and milk and are put to bed by Mercy—and then suddenly turn into "young men and strong", able to fight with a giant and help to destroy Doubting Castle, and become husbands and fathers? The chronology has gone astray, but perhaps these are the defects inseparable from every work of true genius; besides which, John wrote it at intervals, and not straight off. "If you were to polish it," remarks S.T. Coleridge, "you would destroy at once the reality of the vision."

Sometimes Bunyan uses colloquialisms, obsolete words and homely expressions. When the pilgrims get to the top of Hill Difficulty "they were very willing to sit down for they were all in a pelting heat." At the inn, mine host says, "You have gone a good stitch, you may well be a-weary." Their talk is full of proverbs and proverbial expressions. Christian says that the house of Talkative "is as empty of religion as the white of an egg is of savour". The common folk who know Talkative says that he is "a saint abroad and a devil at home". Sometimes Bunyan reverts to the language of his unregenerate days, as Sir Charles Firth points out. Old Mr Honest is described by Greatheart as "a cock of the right kind", a reference to a profane sport in which doubtless John had taken part in old times. In Doubting Castle, when Christian had discovered the key called Promise in his bosom, he found the gate difficult to unlock, for "that the lock went damnable hard". (Some editors of Bunyan have changed the offending word!)

He introduces symbolical sights and pictures which the Pilgrims see in the House Beautiful and elsewhere because they are likely to appeal to readers. The man with the muck-rake, the parlour full of dust, the two little children in their chairs, the robin with the spider in its mouth—all would interest the uneducated and the young.

4

The road on which the various pilgrims travel is realistically described. It is not unlike an old Roman road, straight as a rule, up Hill Difficulty, across the "delicate plain called Ease", onward to the last river and the glorious beyond.

Sometimes there is a high wall with fruit trees beyond to tempt children. Dogs bark as travellers pass, and frighten women; other travellers meet or overtake them; they see men lying asleep by the roadside; they see criminals hanging in irons; they see pleasant green lanes, meadows, styles, bypaths. Indeed the road to the Celestial City is very like a common English seventeenth century road on which Bunyan had wandered and travelled all his life.

Macaulay describes an English road in the time of Charles II. "It was only in fine weather that the whole breadth of the road was available for wheeled vehicles. Often the mud lay deep on the right hand and the left; and only a narrow track of firm ground rose above the quagmire ... It happened almost every day that coaches stuck fast, until a team of cattle could be procured from some neighbouring farm, to tug them out of the slough." This recalls that "very miry slough" called Despond, where Christian and Pliable "wallowed for a time, being grievously bedaubed with the dirt, because they missed the stepping stones in the middle".

There were frequent floods in the seventeenth century. Sometimes coach passengers had to swim for their lives. Christian and Hopeful were surprised in Bye-path meadow by the sudden rising of the river, as no doubt John himself had often been. There was, too, in seventeenth century England, the danger of highwaymen. Their favourite haunting-places were the open heaths and moors around London, or they would lie in wait in woods that bordered the great roads. Mounted highwaymen attacked coaches and horsemen, while poor pedestrians were preyed on by footpads, gangs of sturdy rogues armed with cudgels who assaulted, robbed, and even killed their victims. Such were those who attacked Valiant-for-truth and plundered Little-faith.

Vanity Fair is a scene from the life of the times. With its booths, goods, jugglers, plays, games etc., it was very familiar to John. He had seen the Fair at Elstow, the Great Fair at Stourbridge near Cambridge, and in all probability Bartholomew Fair at Smithfield in London. The Quakers made a habit of preaching at fairs and markets, and maybe Bunyan did likewise. The trial of Christian and Hopeful at Vanity Fair resembles, as Macaulay says, the parody of justice administered by hostile judges to accused Nonconformists. Some of the characters John describes had sat in judgement on himself.

The Pilgrim's Progress is the prose epic of English Puritanism, full of the Puritan's aims, doctrines, and speech. John Bunyan wrote in order to bring men to repentance and faith, not to become an "English man of letters". Yet it stands as a vital part of our religious heritage, and men and women in all parts of the world, and of all ages and classes, have found inspiration and light in its pages.

Before his final release from prison John Bunyan read the manuscript to some of his fellow prisoners. They were divided as to its value. Some thought that it was dangerous to put the Christian life into the form of a romance, but others urged him to print it for it might do good.

> At last I thought, since you are thus divided,
> I print it will, and so the case decided.

No doubt Elizabeth agreed when it was read to her.

5

It came out in a small octavo volume of 326 pages costing one shilling and sixpence. Its success was immediate and John was astonished at it. A second edition appeared the same year, and a third, incorporating some new material, in 1679. No less than eleven editions amounting to 100,000 copies, an enormous sale for the seventeenth century, appeared in his life-time. In July 1926 one of the only few known copies of the first edition was sold for £6,800.

Some years later, perhaps due to the urging of friends, John Bunyan sat down to write the Part Two of *The Pilgrim's Progress*, which was published in 1685 in London by Nicholas Ponder, who had issued Part One. The story of Christiana, her children, and her young companion Mercy is of absorbing interest, though perhaps less dramatic and vivid than the story of Christian. It is also a shade more discursive, as for example in Mr Greatheart's long narrative of Mr Fearing. There is a great variety of characters and incidents both grave and gay. Much sound Puritan doctrine is inculcated in the speeches. Mr Greatheart, Mr Standfast, and Mr Valiant-for-truth represent the stalwart Puritan warriors John had so much admired at Newport Pagnell, and they were his conception of the mature Christian going on pilgrimage. Not one pilgrim fails to get to the Celestial City, though Mr Ready-to-halt gets to the river bank on crutches, and Mr Despondency and his daughter Miss Much-afraid have to be rescued by Mr Greatheart from Giant Despair.

For Mr Valiant-for-truth and Mr Standfast death has no sting and the grave no victory. Mr Standfast's farewell is exceptionally fine: "This River has been a terror to many, yea the thoughts of it also have often frighted me. But now methinks I stand easy, my foot is fixed upon that upon which the feet of the priests that bare the Ark of the Covenant stood while Israel went over Jordan. The waters are indeed to the palate bitter, and to the stomach cold, yet the thoughts of what I am going to, and the conduct that waits for me on the other side, doth lie as a glowing coal to my heart.

"I see myself now at the end of my journey, my toilsome days are ended. I am going now to see that Head that was crowned with thorns, and that Face that was spit upon for me. I have formerly lived by hearsay and faith, but now I go where I shall live by sight, and shall be with Him in whose company I delight myself. I have loved to hear my Lord spoken of, and wherever I have seen the print of His shoe in the earth, there I have coveted to set my foot too. His name has been to me as a civetbox, yea sweeter than all perfumes. His voice to me has been most sweet, and His countenance I have more desired than they that have most desired the light of the sun. His Word I did use to gather for my food, and for antidotes against my faintings. He has held me up, and I have kept me from mine iniquities. Yes, my steps hath He strengthened in His way.

"Now while he was thus in discourse, his countenance changed, his strong man bowed under him and after he had said, 'Take me, for I come unto Thee', he ceased to be seen of them. But glorious it was to see how the open region was filled with horses and chariots, with trumpeters and pipers, with singers and players on stringed instruments, to welcome the Pilgrims as they went up, and followed one another in at the beautiful gate of the City."

This passage, and many like it in both parts of *The Pilgrim's Progress* have been a comfort and a strength to multitudes of pilgrims on the same heavenly road. And with man's nature unchanging, and the grace of God in Christ eternally the same, the book will continue to speak to the soul of man until the end of time.

10

Eager Writer

John Bunyan was the author of more than sixty works, ranging from slim pamphlets to books of considerable size. When he first realised that he had the ability to express himself in print his pen was that of a ready writer. Many of the earlier works were on controversial topics, but they will repay study. The later works, more mature in tone, include the great allegories, but all are true to his understanding of the Christian faith as he found it taught in Scripture. The books written in verse we shall consider in the next chapter. Here we shall survey the less familiar works in summary fashion, and the other two great allegories in more detail.

1

We have already briefly noted John's earliest controversial works against Quaker doctrine. His fourth book, written before his imprisonment, was *The Doctrine of the Law and Grace Unfolded*; the title page added, "Published by that poor and contemptible creature, John Bunyan of Bedford". It was issued in 1659 by M. Wright, "at the sign of the King's Head in the Old Bailey", and also by his friend Matthias Cowley at Newport Pagnell. It is an exposition of Romans 6,14—"Sin shall not have dominion over you: for ye are not under the law, but under grace'', a favourite theme with him. Like many of his shorter works it was no doubt a sermon enlarged for publication. John used notes in preaching, and his prodigious memory enabled him to recall the discourse as well as to add to it. He describes the covenant of works, under which man, a sinner, is obliged to keep the law of God. This he is unable perfectly to do. In contrast, the believer is under a new covenant of grace, made with Christ. He told the story of his early struggles, and how he had seen ''through grace that it was the blood shed on Mount Calvary that did save and redeem sinners, as clearly and as really with the eyes of my soul as ever methought I had seen a penny-loaf bought with a penny.''

His next book, *A Discourse Touching Prayer* (1662) contained the substance of a prison sermon in which he pleaded for spontaneity in prayer as against formalism. The Holy Spirit alone assists men to pray. The Book of Common Prayer, he says, being a merely human invention, cannot do it. In this he is scarcely fair, since Archbishop Cranmer and other reformers compiled the book under the guidance of the Spirit, and it has been helpful to multitudes. And he says, ''You will find those that plead for the Spirit of prayer in the gaol, and them that look after the form of men's inventions only in the alehouse''—not one of Bunyan's happier statements, and quite untrue as regards many.

The year 1664 was occupied with two volumes—*The Holy City*, and *The Resurrection of the Dead, and Eternal Judgement*. The first was a prison address. ''Upon a certain first day, (i.e. Sunday; he is adopting Quaker usage!) I being together with my brethren in our prison chamber, they expected that according to our custom, something should be spoken out of the Word for our mutual edification; but at that time I felt myself, it being my turn to speak, so empty, spiritless, and barren, that I thought I should not have been able to speak among them so much as five words of truth with life and evidence.'' But the Lord, as always, came to the rescue. There came into his mind a vision of the Holy City spoken of in Revelation 21 and 22, and he preached his sermon, his first glorious dream of the Celestial City, and refreshing to them all. In it he said, "In the end it shall not be as now, a Popish doctrine, a Quaker's doctrine, a Prelatical doctrine, and the Presbyter, Independent, and Anabaptist thus distinguished, and thus confounded and destroying. Then the City is of pure gold, as showing how invincible and unconquerable is the spirit of the people of God."

The Resurrection of the Dead was based on Acts 24:14-15, in which he contrasts those who are "dead in sin" with those "alive in Christ", and their eternal rewards. This was published by Francis Smith in London in 1665, and for long made a great impression, though much of it would not meet the taste of today.

2

Grace Abounding to the Chief of Sinners , published by George Larkin in London in 1666, we have already noted and quoted from. This spiritual Autobiography is of the same order as the *Confessions* of Augustine, Thomas a Kempis, *Imitation of Christ,* and in our own time, *In Search of Myself* by D.R. Davies. How long it took to write we cannot tell, but to his prodigious memory we owe the record of God's dealing with him in grace, of his preaching, and later in an addition, the record of his arrest and trial. It tells us practically nothing of his education, army life, marriages, and family, things we would dearly love to know. It is clear as we read that John Bunyan has grown in stature since his first setting out on the pilgrim road, to mature conviction and grasp of Christian truth and ways. "I could have enlarged much in this my discourse of my temptations and troubles for sin," he says in his Preface, "I could also have stepped into a style much higher than this, but I dare not. God did not play in tempting of me; neither did I play when I sunk as into a bottomless pit, when the pangs of Hell caught hold upon me; wherefore I may not play in relating of them, but be plain and simple, and lay down the thing as it was." He urges his readers to call to mind the former days when God laid hold of them in his grace. "It is profitable for Christians to be often calling to mind the very beginnings of Grace with their souls ... Have you forgotten the close, the milk-house, the stable, the barn and the like, where God did visit your souls? ... If you have sinned against the light, if you are tempted to blaspheme, if you are down in despair, if you think God fights against you, or if Heaven is hid from your eyes, remember it was thus with me; but out of them all the Lord delivered me." The experiences he records in *Grace Abounding* are seen in the characters of *The Pilgrim's Progress*, and there is little doubt that he could not have written the great allegory had he not experienced God's saving mercy recounted in the autobiography. It has an undying vitality and perpetual youth about it, is a record of Puritan experience unsurpassed, and a spiritual stimulus of great value. *The Continuation of Mr Bunyan's Life* added to *Grace Abounding* is thought to have been written by George Cokayne, John's old friend from Cotton End, but later Pastor of a church in Red Cross Street, London, and one of those who were with him when he died.

3

As has been shown there was a six year interval between the writing of *Grace Abounding* (1666), and his next book, *A Confession of my Faith* in 1672. Back in prison after his short respite at home he determined to write a book about the principles for which he had been in prison so long. The full title is, *A Confession of my Faith; And a Reason for my Practice; or with who, and who not, I can hold Church-Fellowship, or the Communion of Saints*. George Offer in his *Complete Works of John Bunyan* in three volumes, entitles the book, *Bunyan on the Terms of Communion*, not an improvement on the original, and adds to it two other works, *Differences in Judgement about Water Baptism no Bar to Communion*, and *Peaceable Principles and True*. In *A Confession of my Faith* he reiterates his belief in God, The Trinity, the Deity of Christ, and writes of justification, repentance, faith, and other elements of the Christian faith.

With regard to baptism he writes, "I speak to persuade my brethren of the baptized way, not to make it an essential of the Gospel of Christ, nor yet the communion of saints." For this he was violently attacked by three leading strict Baptists of London, Paul, D'Anvers, and Kiffin, to whom he replied in the second part concerning water baptism. Faith and holiness, he tells them, and not water baptism are the essential basis of a church. Christ, not baptism, is the way to the sheep fold. Not all New Testament saints were baptized. Baptists are divisive of the Church. "Show me the man that is a visible believer, and although he differ with me about baptism, the doors of the church stand open for him." Interestingly enough, at the very time he was in controversy with the London men concerning baptism, Elizabeth Bunyan took her son Joseph to be christened at St Cuthbert's Church. She evidently remained an Anglican, and John made no objection. He was all for toleration on matters of little importance.

In 1674, the year of the deaths of Milton and Clarendon, John published a further reply to Paul and D'Anvers entitled, *Peaceable Principles and True*. In this he repeats many of his previous arguments, but also says, "I know none to whom the title of Baptist is so proper as to the disciples of John (the Baptist). And since you would know by what name I would be distinguished from others, I tell you I would be, and I hope I am, a Christian ... And as for those factious titles of Anabaptists, Independents, Presbyterians or the like, I conclude that they come neither from Jerusalem, nor Antioch, but rather from hell and Babylon, for they naturally tend to divisions."

4

A book which greatly annoyed him came into his hands sometime in 1672. This was *The Design of Christianity* by Edward Fowler, published the previous year. Fowler had been one of the ejected clergy who in 1662 refused to accept the terms of the Act of Uniformity. Subsequently he conformed, and ended as Bishop of Gloucester. He is said to have inspired the character of Mr Worldly-Wiseman, added to the second edition of *The Pilgrim's Progress*. Fowler's *Design* was intended to show that Christianity is meant to restore man to his original state before the Fall, and that by the exercise of his own righteousness or good works. Bunyan took forty-two days to answer this book, which he showed to be contrary to Scripture and to the Thirty-Nine Articles of the Church of England. He gives a careful statement of the Reformed doctrine of Justification by Faith only, which he had learned long ago from Martin Luther. Living faith is essential to salvation. Fowler replied with an abusive book entitled *Dirt Wip't Off*, about which the less said the better. John ignored it.

His next book, *Light for Them that Sit in Darkness*, an elaboration of one of his sermons, was published in 1674. His object was to prove that all our knowledge of the Saviour must be received directly from the written Word; that Christ took on himself our nature, and by his perfect obedience to the Law and making a sin-atoning sacrifice of himself, paid the full price of man's redemption.

While he was on the run before his arrest in the autumn of 1676, he wrote a catechism entitled, *Instructions for the Ignorant*, probably while hidden in the home of a friend. He addresses the Bedford Church and speaks of himself as "being driven from you in presence not affection". It was issued in 1675.

Next came his twenty-fifth publication, *Saved by Grace*, (1675), in which he went over familiar ground. What it is to be saved, what grace is, who are saved by grace—only the contrite and needy, and the proofs of their salvation.

The following year, 1676, Francis Smith of London brought out Bunyan's *The Strait Gate, or the great Difficulty of Going to Heaven*. It is an expanded version of a sermon on Luke 13:24, going over much the same ground as *Saved by Grace*.

Come and Welcome to Jesus Christ, published in 1678 the year of *The Pilgrim's Progress*, and based on John 6:37

became one of the most popular books he wrote, several editions appearing in his lifetime. It has often been reprinted in our own day. In it Bunyan seeks to show the cause, truth, and manner of the coming of a sinner to Christ, and of his reception and blessings when he comes. This was followed in 1679 by *A Treatise on the Fear of God*, in the best Puritan style of many divisions and subdivisions.

5

The Life and Death of Mr. Badman, the third of Bunyan's major works, appeared in 1680, two years after the Part One of *The Pilgrim's Progress*. A strong tradition says that he wrote it at Bocking End in Essex, in a farmhouse belonging to John English, an elder of Bocking Independent Meeting. In the intervals of writing it he preached to hundreds of Essex Nonconformists in the great barn of the farm. *The Life and Death of Mr. Badman* was intended to be the counter-part of *The Pilgrim's Progress*, and to show an evil man on the road to hell. Some features of the man Wildman who had so troubled the Bedford Meeting are enshrined in the character of Mr. Badman, and doubtless many characteristics of others whom John had met. The story does not approach the gripping liveliness of *The Pilgrim's Progress*, and the narrative is rather slow since it takes the form of a dialogue between Mr. Wiseman and Mr. Attentive. Nevertheless it is very readable, and contains a variety of fascinating anecdotes.

Mr. Badman was "a master-sinner from a childe" much addicted to lying (as John had been), and also to thieving, and even thought that robbing his parents was no crime. He hated the Lord's Day. He is apprenticed to a master, but to what trade we are not told. He robs his master and frequents ale-houses, and gets "as drunk as a beast" very often. Then he marries a virtuous orphan for her money, breaks her heart with his misconduct, defrauds his creditors by a sham bankruptcy, emerges more prosperous than ever, and finally, through a second marriage—with a woman as worthless as himself, loses everything. But how, it may be asked, does such a man die? Bunyan tells us—"as quietly as a lamb", and leaves us to ponder the destiny of the finally impenitent. "They are bad men that make bad times", Mr. Wiseman remarks to Mr. Attentive; "if men therefore would mend, so would the times."

6

The fourth of Bunyan's major works, *The Holy War*, appeared in 1682, and is second only to *The Pilgrim's Progress* in interest and fascination. Macaulay expressed the opinion that it would be England's greatest religious allegory if *The Pilgrim's Progress* had never been written. The full title is *The Holy War, made by Shaddai upon Diabolus for the Regaining of the Metropolis of the World, Or, The Losing and Taking Again of the Town of Mansoul*. George Offer remarks that he had studied the book for more than fifty years, and announces it to be a solemn, soul-stirring, and delightful narrative. Which it is. It is a great pity that this grand book is not better known.

The story sets out to recall the fall and redemption of mankind under the guise of a besieged city. The city of Mansoul originally belonged by right to Shaddai or God, but was betrayed through Ear Gate and Eye Gate into the hands of Diabolus or the Devil, the besieging giant who takes control. In the hands of the enemy Mansoul loses its Mayor, Lord Understanding, and Mr. Conscience is dismissed from his post as Recorder. Lord Will-be-will becomes the Lord of Mansoul—man's fallen will, self-will, and ill-will all combined in one unpleasant and anti-God character. *The Pilgrim's Progress* sets forth the spiritual life under the Scriptural figure of a long and uphill journey. *The Holy War*, on the other hand, is a military history, full of soldiers and battles, defeats and victories. The author's own experiences in the Civil War taught him many memorable things of the military art, and stamped on his mind many marches, sieges, fights and captures which he uses in the story. The characters, too, are very human, and those whom John knew from time to time. Old Mr. Prejudice, an angry and unhappy churl; Captain Anything, who came from a titled family whose crest was a weather-cock, and who was marked by opportunism, insincerity and deceit; stiff old Mr Loth-to-stoop; Ill-pause, the Devil's orator, a treacherous villain if ever there was one; young Captain Self-denial, an officer in Emmanuel's army who overcomes his great enemy Self-love and hangs him on the gallows at the market-cross; Mr. Humble, the juryman, and Miss Humblemind the servant maid; Master Thinkwell, only son of old Mr. Meditation, and Mr. God's-peace, a godly person—we meet them all in *The Holy War*. We are introduced also to a Fast-day in Mansoul, and to a Feast-day, to Emmanuel's livery, all in white, and to Mansoul's Magna Charta—full, free, and everlasting forgiveness, the holy law, grace, and goodness of Emmanuel himself. Mansoul, in the end, is recaptured by Emmanuel's forces, and Diabolus driven out.

In Elstow Church is a Memorial window to *The Holy War*, and beneath it the lines:

> To the Memory of Bunyan,
> And to remind all Christian People
> Of The Holy War they should be engaged in
> On the side of Emmanuel.

Bunyan would have liked that.

Vera Brittain thinks that in *The Holy War* Bunyan satirized the politics of his day. Nothing, surely, was further from his thoughts. He never had much interest in politics. He had only to look into his own soul, with the light of Scripture, and consider the way in which apostate and unbelieving men are brought back to God, to have the entire conflict in *The Holy War* before his eyes.

7

After the publication of *The Holy War* in 1682 Bunyan wrote six short books before continuing the story of the pilgrims in Part Two of *The Pilgrim's Progress*, published in 1685. *The Barren Fig-Tree* is an exposition of the parable in Luke 13. *The Greatness of the Soul*, published in 1683, is a sermon he preached in London at Pinner's Hall. In that year he also wrote, *A Case of Conscience Resolved*, an answer to an enquiry from some London women as to whether they should meet to pray separately from their men. John's answer is a decided "No", but today his answer would be very different! In April 1684 appeared a poem, *A Caution to Stir up to Watch against Sin*. This was followed, that same year, by *A Holy Life, the Beauty of Christianity,* also by *Seasonable Counsel, or Advice to Sufferers*—these being those persecuted for righteousness sake. They are bidden to trust in God, but he includes a statement of loyalty to king and government.

In 1685 came *The Perpetuity of the Seventh-day Sabbath*, which need not detain us, and *The Pharisee and the Publican* expounding the parable. The next year came, *A Book for Boys and Girls* in verse, which will be considered in the next chapter.

1688, the year of John Bunyan's death, saw no fewer than five publications from his pen. *The Jerusalem Sinner Saved, or Good News for the Vilest of Men* speaks of the great mercy of Christ to all kinds of sinners. This book has always been a favourite with lovers of Bunyan, and has a message for us still. Its immediate successor, *The Work of Jesus Christ as an Advocate*, also an expanded sermon, shows the necessity of Christ's work an as advocate for the believer, and the benefits his advocacy brings. *The Water of Life*, and *Solomon's Temple Spiritualized* are both sermons describing the grace and glory of God. The manuscript of *The Acceptable Sacrifice* he had in his pocket on his last journey to London, and it was published after his death. It is a discourse on the nature, signs, and proper effects of a contrite heart. Also published in 1689 was John Bunyan's last sermon on John 1:13, *Which were born, not of blood, nor of the will of the flesh, nor of the will of man, but of God*, a true Calvinist sermon, very typical of the preacher.

After Bunyan's death, Charles Doe visited Elizabeth at Bedford and received from her various manuscripts, chiefly sermons, already prepared by John for the press. These he collected and issued in a Folio in 1692. They consist of the following: *An Exposition of the Ten First Chapters of Genesis; Of Justification by Imputed Righteousness; Paul's Departure and Crown; Of the Trinity and a Christian; Of the Law and a Christian; Israel's Hope Encouraged; The Desires of the Righteous Granted; The Saint's Privilege and Profit; Christ a Complete Saviour; The Saint's Knowledge of Christ's Love; The House of the Forest of Lebanon;* and *Of Antichrist and His Ruin*. Later, in 1698, Charles Doe published *The Heavenly Footman*, consisting of nine directions to those who run for Heaven. It is addressed to "slothful and careless people". "The Cross," wrote Bunyan, "is the standing way-mark by which all they that go to glory must pass by." He had found it to be so himself, long years before, and it had been central to all his preaching and teaching.

A good deal of the writing of John Bunyan will not be to the taste of modern readers, but those who are willing to try will find that reading his minor works can bring much spiritual profit and illumination.

11

Maker of Verses

1

Throughout his many books John Bunyan produced a considerable amount of verse. It would be too much to assert that it is true poetry, though it is fair to say that he had a better idea of verse structure than many over-praised poets writing today. Southey thought that the practice of writing verse was inspired by reading Foxe's *Book of Martyrs* in which there is some verse. Even where his verse is little more than doggerel it contains original thought, and some of his lines are memorable. Verse was not his natural medium, but with the fine imagination shown in his great allegories he had a faculty which, with more education and knowledge of literature, might have made him a poet indeed. There is a poet's touch in the lines in his *Book for Boys and Girls* beginning:—

> "A comely sight indeed it is to see
> A world of blossom on an apple tree"

reminiscent of W.H. Davies.

The Oxford Book of Verse includes his "Christiana's song":

Blest be the day that I began
  A pilgrim for to be,
And blessed also be that man
  That thereto moved me.

'Tis true, 'twas long ere I began
  To seek to live for ever:
But now I run fast as I can:
  'Tis better late than never.

Another of his pilgrim songs, much loved though sadly altered in some hymn-books, was sung most appropriately at the funeral of Sir Winston Churchill:

Who would true valour see
  Let him come hither;
One here will constant be,
  Come wind, come weather.
There's no discouragement
Shall make him once relent
His first avowed intent
  To be a pilgrim.

Who so beset him round
  With dismal stories,
Do but themselves confound;
  His strength the more is.
No lion can him fright,
He'll with a giant fight,
But he will have a right
  To be a pilgrim.

Hobgoblin nor foul fiend
  Can daunt his spirit;
He knows he at the end
  Shall life inherit.
Then fancies fly away,
He'll fear not what men say,
He'll labour night and day
  To be a pilgrim.

Some have seen in this an echo of the song in Shakespeare's *As You Like It*, Act 2, scene 5—"Who doth ambition shun." There is no evidence that Bunyan was acquainted with

Shakespeare's plays, and the metrical schemes of his verses and those of Shakespeare are very different.

Mr Greatheart heard with much enjoyment the song of the shepherd boy, and so do we:

> He that is down needs fear no fall,
>   He that is low no pride;
> He that is humble ever shall
>   Have God to be his guide.
>
> I am content with what I have,
>   Little be it or much;
> Lord, contentment still I crave
>   Because thou savest such.
>
> Fulness to such a burden is
>   That go on pilgrimage;
> Here little, and hereafter bliss
>   Is best from age to age.

2

One of Bunyan's first literary works from prison, entitled *Prison Meditations*, was in verse, published in 1665. It begins:

> Friend, I salute thee in the Lord,
>   And wish thou may'st abound
> In faith, and have a good regard
>   To keep on holy ground.

It consists of seventy four-line stanzas.

> I am, indeed, in prison now
>   In body, but my mind
> Is free to study Christ, and how
>   Unto me He is kind.
>
> Here dwells good conscience, also peace
>   Here be my garments white;
> Here, though in bonds, I have release
>   From guilt, which else would bite.

He turns on his persecutors:

For all your spirits are so stout,
  For matters that are vain;
Your sin besets you round about,
  You are in Satan's chain.

On the other hand God's people conquer and are blessed.

Also from prison he issued *One Thing Is Needful,* meditations on Death, Judgement, Heaven and Hell (1664) in no less than 296 rhymed quatrains. This was followed by *Ebal and Gerizim,* a long doctrinal treatise in rhymed couplets, unlikely to grip readers today.

3

After this John gave up writing verse for a considerable time, perhaps discouraged by the comments of some of his more learned fellow-prisoners. But in *The Pilgrim's Progress* he reverts to it, and we are glad he did. "The Author's Apology for his Book" is in rhymed couplets:

When at the first I took my pen in hand,
Thus for to write; I did not understand
That I at all should make a little book
In such a mode; Nay, I had undertook
To make another, which when almost done,
Before I was aware, I this begun.
  And thus it was: I writing of the way
And race of Saints, in this our Gospel-day,
Fell suddenly into an Allegory
About their journey, and the way to Glory,
In more than twenty things, which I set down;
This done, I twenty more had in my crown,
And they again began to multiply,
Like sparks that from the coals of fire do fly ...

Later on he says,

> This book will make a traveller of thee,
> If by its counsel thou wilt ruled be;
> It will direct thee to the Holy Land,
> If thou wilt its directions understand:
> Yea, it will make the slothful, active be;
> The blind also, delightful things to see.

and he concludes what by any standards is a remarkable prologue—

> Would'st thou be in a Dream, and yet not sleep?
> Or wouldest thou in a moment laugh, and weep?
> Wouldest thou loose thyself, and catch no harm?
> And find thyself again without a charm?
> Would'st read thyself, and read thou know'st not what
> And yet know whether thou art blest or not,
> By reading the same lines? O then come hither,
> And lay my Book, thy Head, and Heart together.

Christian, when his burden is taken off, goes on singing:

> Thus far did I come loaden with my sin;
> Nor could ought ease the grief that I was in,
> Till I came hither: What a place is this!
> Must here be the beginning of my bliss!
> Must here the burden fall from off my back?
> Must here the strings that bound it to me crack?
> Blest Cross! Blest Sepulchre! blest rather be
> The Man that there was put to shame for me.

Going up the narrow way over Hill Difficulty he says,

> This hill, though high, I covet to ascend;
> The difficulty will not me offend,
> For I perceive the way to life lies here;
> Come, pluck up, heart; let's neither faint nor fear:
> Better, though difficult, th'right way to go,
> Than wrong, though easy, where the end is woe.

Passing the cave where Giants Pope and Pagan dwell, Christian bursts into song:

O world of wonders! (I can say no less)
That I should be preserv'd in that distress
That I have met with here! O blessed be
That hand that from it hath delivered me!
Dangers in darkness, devils, hell and sin,
Did compass me, while I this vale was in:
Yea, snares and pits and traps, and nets did lie
My path about, that worthless silly I
Might have been cach't, intangled, and cast down:
But since I live, let Jesus wear the Crown.

Commenting on the shepherds on the Delectable mountains, whose names were Knowledge, Experience, Watchful and Sincere, he says:

Thus by the shepherds, secrets are revealed,
Which from all other men are kept conceal'd:
Come to the shepherds, then, if you would see
Things deep, things hid, and that mysterious be.

He writes a conclusion to the First Part of *The Pilgrim's Progress*, in which he urges his readers to

Put by the curtains, look within my vail;
Turn up my metaphors and do not fail
There, if thou seekest them, such things to find,
As will be helpful to an honest mind.

Part Two of the great book begins with a long introduction in rhymed couplets in which he introduces some of the characters, in order to whet the appetites of those who have read the First Part.

Go, now my little Book, to every place
Where my first Pilgrim has but shown his face:
Call at their door: If any say, who's there?
Then answer thou, Christiana is here.
If they bid thee come in, then enter thou
With all thy boys ....

When the women leave the Interpreter's House they sing.

This place has been our second stage,
Here we have heard and seen
Those good things that from age to age,
To others hid have been ...

To move me for to watch and pray,
To strive to be sincere,
To take my cross up day by day,
And serve the Lord wiith fear.

Other verses of varying merit are scattered throughout the book.

4

The *Book for Boys and Girls,* or *Country Rhimes for Children in verse on seventy-four things,* was published in May 1686. Subsequently the title was changed to *Divine Emblems, or Temporal Things Spiritualised.* In 1635 Francis Quarles had published his *Emblems,* paraphrases in verse from the Scriptures, and John may well have read this, perhaps in the bookshop of Matthias Cowley. His own book is a collection of whimsical verse, meditations upon an egg, a bee, a candle, a whipping top, a penny loaf, a looking glass, a frog, a snail etc. Although probably not to the taste of children today they no doubt lightened the Sabbath for many a little Puritan. One of the best poems in the collection is "The Child with the bird:

My little bird, how canst thou sit
  And sing amidst so many thorns?
  Let me a hold upon thee get,
My love with honour thee adorns.

Thou art at present little worth;
  Five farthings none will give for thee;
But prythee, little bird, come forth;
  Thou of more value art to me.

'Tis true, it is sunshine today;
  Tomorrow birds will have a storm.
My pretty one, come thou away;
  My bosom then shall keep thee warm.

Thou subject art to cold o'nights
  When darkness is thy covering;
At days thy danger's great by kites;
  How canst thou then sit there and sing?

Thy food is scarce and scanty, too;
  'Tis worms and trash which thou dost eat;
Thy present state I pity do;
  Come, I'll provide thee better meat.

I'll feed thee with white bread and milk
  And sugar plums, if them thou crave;
I'll cover thee with finest silk,
  That from the cold I may thee save.

....

I'll keep thee safe from cat and cur;
  No manner o'harm shall come to thee;
Yea, I will be thy succourer,
  My bosom shall thy cabin be.

But lo, behold, the bird is gone;
  These charmings would not make her yield;
The child's left at the bush alone;
  The bird flies yonder o'er the field.

There is quite a vivid description in the clash between the fly and the candle:

To clash at light? Away, thou silly fly!
Thus, doing thou wilt burn thy wings and die.
But 'tis a folly her advice to give;
She'll kill the candle, or she will not live.
Slap, says she, at it! Then she makes retreat,
So wheels about, and doth her blows repeat!

A country scene suggests *The Lark and the Fowler* which has all the simplicity of a true parable:

Thou simple bird, what makes thee here to play?
Look, there's the fowler! prythee come away.
Dost not behold the net? Look there, 'tis spread;
Venture a little further, thou art dead.
Is there not room enough in all the field
For thee to play in, but thou needs must yield
To the deceitful glitt'ring of a glass,
Placed betwixt nets to bring thy death to pass?
Bird, if thou art so much for dazzling light,
Look, there's the sun above thee; dart upright!
Thy nature is to soar up to the sky:
Why wilt thou come down to the nets and die?

The emblem upon the beggar points a moral:

He wants, he asks, he pleads his poverty.
They within doors do him an alms deny.
He doth repeat and aggravate his grief;
But they repulse him, give him no relief.
He begs: they say 'Begone!' he will not hear,
He coughs and sighs, to show he still is there;
They disregard him, he repeats his groans;
They still say 'Nay' and he himself bemoans.
They call him 'Vagrant', and more rugged grow;
He cries the shriller; trumpets out his woe.
At last, when they perceive he'll take no nay,
An alms they give him, without more delay.
The beggar doth resemble them that pray

To God for mercy, and will take no nay;
But wait, and count that all His hard gainsays
Are nothing else but fatherly delays;
Then imitate him, praying souls, and cry,
There's nothing like to importunity.

His "Meditations upon an Egg" is also full of similes:

The egg's no chick by falling from a hen,
Nor man's a Christian till he's born again;
The egg's at first contained in the shell,
Men afore grace in sin and darkness dwell;
The egg, when laid, by warmth is made a chicken,
And Christ by grace the dead in sin doth quicken;
The egg when first a chick the shell's its prison,
So flesh to soul who yet with Christ is risen ....

Of a swallow he writes:

This pretty bird! Oh, how she flies and sings;
But could she do so if she had not wings?
Her wings bespeake my faith, her songs my peace;
When I believe and sing, my doubtings cease.

His "Meditations upon a Candle" is quite a long poetical effort, and he draws many parallels between candles and Christians. Here is the first verse:

A man's like a candle in a candlestick,
Made up of tallow and a little wick;
For what the candle is, before its lighted,
Just such be they who are in sin benighted.
Nor can a man his soul with grace inspire,
More than the candles set themselves on fire.
Candles receive their light from what they are not;
Men grace from Him, for whom at first they care not.
We manage candles when they take the fire;
God men, when He with grace doth them inspire.

His book of verses for children is a kind and loving book, with great understanding of a child's interests, and only once does he sound a stern note in "The Disobedient Child."

They snap and snarl, if Parents them controul,
Tho but in things most hurtful to the soul.
They reckon they are Masters, and that we
Who parents are, should to them subjects be!
They'll by wrong doings, under parents, gather
And say, it is no sin to rob a father.
They'll jostle parents out of place and power,
They'll make themselves the Head, and them devour.

In his preface to *The Holy War*, written in verse, Bunyan says,

I saw the prince's armed men come down
By troops, by thousands, to besiege the town.
I saw the captains, heard the trumpets sound,
And how his forces covered all the ground.
Yea, how they set themselves in battle-'ray
I shall remember to my dying day.

Here, surely is a reminiscence of his days as a soldier under Fairfax, perhaps even of the Battle of Naseby.

Although John Bunyan was no poet there is much value in many of his best verses. Typical of these are his versifying of the Christian's armour as set forth in Ephesians 6:

This is the man death cannot kill,
  For he hath put on arms;
Him sin nor Satan hath not skill
  To hurt with all their charms.

A helmet on his head doth stand,
  A breastplate on his heart;
A shield also is in his hand,
  That blunteth every dart.

Truth girds him round the reins, also
  His sword is on his thigh;
His feet in shoes of peace do go
  The ways of purity.

His heart it groaneth to the Lord,
  Who hears him at his call,
And doth him help and strength afford
  Wherwith he conquers all.

Thus fortified he keeps the fields
  While Death is gone and fled;
And then lies down upon his shield
  Till Christ doth raise the dead.

12

Triumphant Years

John Bunyan was finally released from Bedford County Gaol in 1677, and had before him just over ten more years of life. They were years of triumph. The story of his courage in imprisonment, the outstanding success of his preaching, and his reputation as a popular author all combined to make him one of the best known and loved men amongst the Nonconformists and even beyond their ranks. His remaining years were full of a variety of activities after his own heart, in which he strove to serve his Master.

1

His father, Thomas Bunyan, died in the cottage at Harrowden in February 1676. In his will he left one shilling each to his sons John and Thomas and his daughters Mary and Elizabeth, while the rest of his goods went to his third wife Anne, who survived him for four years. He seems to have come round to his son John's way of thinking, for he bequeathed his soul "into the hands of Almighty God my Maker, hoping that through the meritorious death and passion of Jesus Christ my only Saviour and Redeemer to receive pardon for my sins."

Charles II died in 1685, a declared Roman Catholic, with a

numerous progeny by his many mistresses, but none of them legitimate. His brother, James II, a staunch and open Roman Catholic for many years, ascended the throne. He believed it possible that the Church of England could be persuaded to favour Romanism because of its opposition to Protestant Nonconformity. It was an illusion. The new Parliament of May 1685 met with determination to resist both Romanism and Dissent. In July came Monmouth's rebellion. James, Duke of Monmouth, a son of Charles I, and a Protestant, attempted to overthrow the new regime in the interests of Protestantism. Six thousand men rallied to his cause in the West of England, many of them Nonconformists, but the rising was poorly organized and equipped and easily suppressed. Then followed the "Bloody Assize" of Chief Justice Jeffreys, who hanged three hundred and fifty rebels without mercy. This cruelty was heartily supported by the king. Two of Kiffin's grandsons perished, in spite of the generous financial support he had given to Charles II. The whole country was stirred and apprehensive. What fresh troubles might ensue? Non-conformists especially began to prepare for the worst.

John Bunyan decided to draw up a "Deed of Gift" which would confer on Elizabeth all his worldly goods, so that should he be arrested once more she would not be penniless. This deed, in John's handwriting, was drawn up on the 23rd December 1685 and witnessed by four members of the Bedford Church. It begins— "To all people to whom this present writing shall come, I, John Bunyan of the parish of St Cuthberts, in the town of Bedford, Brazier, send greeting. Know ye that I, the said John Bunyan, as well for and in consideration of the natural affection and love which I have and bear unto my well-beloved wife, Elizabeth, as also for divers other good causes and considerations me at this present especially moving, have given and granted ... all and singular my goods, chattels, debts, ready money, plate, rings, household stuff, apparel, utensils, brass, pewter, bedding, and all other my substance whatsoever ..." This document was not his will, as it has been regarded. It was a document to insure that his goods could not be illegally seized should he be arrested or fined for any reason. Because of the troubled times John hid it in the thatched roof of his house, and not even Elizabeth seems to have known where it was. On his death it was so securely hidden that it could not be found, and his wife was obliged to administer John's estate as that of an intestate person. In 1838, when the house was pulled down, the document was discovered, and is now in the possession of the Bunyan Meeting, Bedford.

James II gave authority for avowed Romanists among the clergy to keep their benefices. Such men became deans and bishops and members of the Roman Church were also appointed to major posts in the Army. When members of the Franciscan and Carmelite Orders began to walk openly in London, and mass to be celebrated, there were riots in the city. James made a bid for support by issuing in April 1687 a new Declaration of Indulgence which suspended all penal laws against Catholics and Nonconformists alike. This action alarmed the Established clergy.

2

Against this background of unrest and uncertainty John Bunyan pursued his vigorous way. The writer who wrote the *Continuation of Grace Abounding* described him as "tall of stature, strong boned, though not corpulent, somewhat of a ruddy face, with sparkling eyes, wearing his hair on his upper lip after the old British fashion; his hair reddish, but in his latter days time had sprinkled it with grey; his nose well set, but not declining or bending, and his mouth moderate large; his forehead something high, and his habit (i.e. clothes) always plain and modest."

He was in good health and was constantly out and about preaching to the associated congregations of the Bedford Church, as well as expounding Scripture in the mother church, and going to distant places on horse-back. There was, too, the pastoral work of visitation, and the preparing of his writings for the press. He preached at Reading,

Hitchin, Aylesbury, Luton, Leicester, and many other places. He went frequently to London where he had large and appreciative congregations, and made many friends. On one of his visits he stayed with friends who occupied one of the many houses then built on London Bridge itself. The city, containing half a million people, enthralled him, but he was always glad to get back to Bedford. He was offered the pastorate of a leading London Nonconformist Church, but declined it, although it would have provided a much better income for him and Elizabeth. He would see springing up in the capital, the new coffee-houses which were beginning to serve tea also. He would be amazed at the fashions of the gaily dressed girls, and at the dandified garments of the men—so different from the clothes worn in days of the Commonwealth. It was six years after the Great Fire of 1666, and everywhere new buildings was in progress, including the new St Paul's—where years later his hymn, "Who would true valour see" would be sung.

The Nonconformists worshipped in many of the halls of the great City Companies, before their own chapels were built. Pinners' Hall, Girdlers' Hall, Salters' Hall were among them, and in these Bunyan was a welcome preacher. In 1677 the Independents founded a Tuesday morning lecture in Pinners' Hall, at which leading divines preached, John Bunyan among them. One of his best sermons, "The Greatness of the Soul", was delivered there in 1688.

Charles Doe recorded the enthusiasm of the common-folk to hear Bunyan preach. "When Mr Bunyan preached in London, if there were but one day's notice given, there would be more people come together to hear him preach than the meeting-house could hold. I have seen to hear him preach, by my computation, about twelve hundred at a morning lecture by seven o'clock on a working day in the dark winter-time. I also computed about three thousand that came to hear him on Lord's Day at London, at a town-end's meeting-house, so that half were fain to go back again for want of room, and then himself was fain at a back-door to be pulled almost over people to get upstairs to his pulpit."

One of his London friends who was greatly attached to him was Sir John Shorter, Lord Mayor of London in 1687, an eminent goldsmith and firm friend of Nonconformists. He established a meeting in Grocers' Hall at which Bunyan often preached. Sir John gave him an ivory-headed staff, and a small inlaid cabinet in which to keep his papers. Their friendship was so close that after his death Bunyan was described as "chaplain to the Lord Mayor", which of course he was not.

Other London friends included Dr. John Owen, the famous Nonconformist divine, who had intervened with Bishop Barlow of Lincoln to secure John's release from his second imprisonment. His congregation met in White's Alley, Moorfields, and there also John preached from time to time, greatly pleasing Dr. Owen with his teaching, upon which he commented favourably to Charles II.

Another friend was George Cokayn, who he had known in Bedfordshire, and who was now pastor of an Independent Congregation in Red Cross Street, in the City of London. John Bunyan preached for him also. In his congregation he met a young grocer of Holborn named John Strudwick with whom he sometimes stayed, and in whose house he was destined to die.

3

One whose friendship he greatly valued was Charles Doe, a comb-maker of Southwark across the river Thames, where Shakespeare had his theatre. He knew John Bunyan only in the last three years of his life, but instantly John became his hero. He had read some of his books and was constrained to hear him preach. He went to a meeting held in a private house. The text was Proverbs 10:24—"The fear of the wicked, it shall come upon him; but the desire of the righteous shall be granted." At first Charles Doe was upset, for he was a New Testament man. But he was to write, "Mr Bunyan went on and preached so New Testament-like that he made me admire, and weep for joy, and give him my affections. And he was the first man that ever I heard preach to my unenlightened understanding and experience, for methought all his sermons were adapted to my condition and had apt similitudes, being full of the lvoe of God and the manner of its secret working upon the soul, and of the soul under the sense of it, that I could weep for joy most part of his sermons; and so by a letter, I introduced myself into his acquaintance, and, indeed, I have not since met with a man I have liked so well. I was acquainted with him but about three years before he died, and then missed him sorely." Doe was so attached to John that after his death he made it his business to search out and publish his unpublished manuscripts.

Bunyan visited his publishers also, such as Nathaniel Ponder and George Larkin, to make arrangements about printing new editions, especially of the allegories. It is not known how much money he received from his various publications, but there must have been some, and it would ease his and Elizabeth's circumstances. His London friends gave him gifts from time to time, but his main support still came from the Bedford Meeting.

One strange fact is that none of John Bunyan's letters seem to have survived. We do not know whether he was much of a letter writer, but he must have written some, concerning his preaching appointments at a distance, to his friends, and to his various publishers. None have so far come to light, though it is possible that some may yet be discovered. Perhaps the uncertain character of the times, together with the Great Fire of London caused their destruction.

The years of the reign of James II were fast running out. Disaffection and incipient rebellion were on every hand. In April 1688 the king ordered a Second Declaration of Indulgence to be read in churches, but hardly a clergyman obeyed. In London Samuel Wesley, the father of John and Charles, preached a sermon on the text, "Be it known unto thee, O king, that we will not serve thy gods, nor worship the golden image which thou hast set up." It met with hearty approval. Seven bishops, including Sancroft, Archbishop of

Canterbury, petitioned against the Indulgence. They were put on trial for seditious libel and acquitted, to the delirious joy of the Londoners, and the general satisfaction of the rest of the country.

During the summer of 1688 many leading English figures passed between England and The Hague, in order to strengthen the design to bring William of Orange who had married James' daughter Mary, to the English throne. William, a staunch Protestant, received an invitation to accept the English crown, supported by the Earls of Shrewsbury, Devonshire, and Danby, Edward Russell of the great House of Bedford, the Marquis of Winchester, Lord Macclesfield, Lord Peterborough, Lord Halifax and many others. The conspiracy planned with great care succeeded. In November Prince William landed at Torbay with thirteen thousand men, and risings occurred simultaneously in the Midlands, Yorkshire, and Scotland. Everywhere the revolt was successful. James, deserted by courtiers and soldiers alike, fled to France. The Protestant succession to the throne, and the Protestant religion were henceforth established in Britain, for the nation saw that the Reformation was something worth maintaining.

John Bunyan did not live to see the "Glorious Revolution" of 1688, though he must have been aware of currents of opinion tending that way, and he may even have had contact with some among the Nonconformists who knew of the plans. Had he lived to see it he would have known that the Puritan struggles of his youth had not been in vain; he would have known that they had laid the foundations in concept and example of constitutional monarchy, free Parliaments, and many of the democratic civil and religious liberties which we enjoy today.

4

While these events were in preparation John Bunyan set out on his last journey. In the middle of August, 1688 he had an engagement to preach in London, but determined to ride by way of Reading to help a young neighbour in trouble. This young man had incurred his father's anger so much that he had threatened to disinherit him, and he asked John to call on his father at Reading and attempt a reconciliation. This John gladly agreed to do, for Christian love and reconciliation was one of the themes he often preached and wrote about. He also had many friends in Reading and the mission would give him a break in his long journey. He had not been well in the Spring, and he was manifestly tired; but although Elizabeth probably sought to deter him from going, he mounted his horse and set off. In his pocket was the manuscript of *The Acceptable Sacrifice, or the Excellency of a Broken Heart* which George Larkin was to publish. In two months' time he would be sixty, but he pressed on with the unshakeable determination which had characterized him from the days of his conversion.

At Reading John stayed with John Rance, pastor of a Meeting House in Mill Lane, and preached there. The next morning he called on the irate father of his young Bedford friend and effected the desired reconciliation. It was nearly midday when he started on the forty-mile ride to London. Before he had got half-way a heavy storm broke and continued with pitiless intensity for some hours. He would have been wise to seek shelter at some inn or roadside house, but for some reason or other he pressed on. Soaked, shivering, and exhausted he reached the house of his friend John Strudwick, the grocer of Snow Hill, Holborn. He was a deacon of the Church presided over by John's friend, George Cokayn. Strudwick and his wife put him to bed and gave him a hot potion of herbs to drink. Next day he was still unwell, and stayed in the house preparing *The Acceptable Sacrifice* for the press. In a day or two he felt better, and on Sunday 19th August he walked with John Strudwick to Whitechapel, a mile away, where in Petticoat Lane John Gammon, an old friend, had his Meeting Place. Here, as he looked on the crowded congregation, much of his old vigour returned, and he preached a powerful sermon on John 1:13. Though he did not know it, it was to be his last.

Two days later, on 21st August, the symptoms of pneumonia appeared, and he retired to bed with a high fever. Although not an old man, his physique had been undermined by years in prison, and overwork in pastoral labours. A doctor was summoned but could do little, with the limited medical knowledge of the day, to help him. He became delirious, and his mind and speech wandered to people and things of far away and long ago. His closest friends, John Strudwick, George Cokayn, John Gammon, and Charles Doe were constantly with him. He probably did not know how ill he was, and how close to the last River of which he had written so superbly. Neither did his friends realize it, or they would have sent for Elizabeth.

John himself did not know of the sudden death of his friend Sir John Shorter, ex-Lord Mayor of London. He had been to open the famous Bartholomew Fair, and returning was on his way to see John Bunyan in his sick room, when, only a few minutes walk from Strudwick's house Sir John was thrown from his horse, and died two or three days later. But John and Sir John certainly met shortly in the Celestial City.

On Friday, 31st August 1688 John Bunyan lay with closed eyes, fighting for breath. He must have realised that he was dying. George Cokayn says that he bore his sufferings "with much constancy and patience; and expressed himself as if he desired nothing more than to be dissolved and to be with Christ ... and resigned his soul into the hands of his most merciful redeemer." And then, a little while later, quietly he died. And for him, too, all the trumpets sounded on the other side!

5

Two days later the sorrowful tidings reached Bedford, a grievous blow to Elizabeth and the children, and painful also to his friends at the Bedford Meeting. William Hawkes, John Gifford's son-in-law, recorded John's death in the Church Book: "Wednesday, 4th of September, was kept in prayer and humiliation for this heavy stroke upon us, the death of dear Brother Bunyan. Appointed also that Wednesday next be kept in prayer and humiliation on the same account." Yet another day, 18th September, was also set aside for the same purpose. John was greatly loved by his people; it was three years before another Pastor was appointed.

On 3rd September 1688 John Bunyan was buried in Bunhill Fields, the City cemetery near Aldersgate. George Cokayn conducted the funeral service in the presence of many mourners all Puritans from London Noncomformist congregations. No doubt he paid a glowing tribute to John's faith, spirit, and writings. Many Dissenters were buried in Bunhill Fields, including John Owen, Daniel Defoe, Isaac Watts, William Blake, Susannah Wesley, mother of John and Charles, and Henry Cromwell, great-great grandson of Oliver. John Strudwick provided a new vault for his dead guest beneath the plane trees. A well-carved effigy of John Bunyan was placed on the tomb in 1861, with sculptured pictures of Christian carrying and losing his burden. In December 1940 and in May 1941 Nazi bombers heavily attacked the City of London and Bunyan's tomb and many others were damaged, but as far as possible the damage has been repaired.

The tinker who in 1650 began housekeeping with his Mary without so much as a dish or spoon between them, was rather better endowed when he died. The Puritan virtues of industry, frugality, and thrift stood him in good stead, as they would us if we practised them. A prolonged search failed to reveal the Deed of gift, and so the administration of his estate was granted to Elizabeth and two of his Bedford friends, Thomas Woodward, Maltster, and William Nichols, Draper. So to her came "all and singular my goods, chattels, debts, ready money, plate, rings, household stuff, apparel, utensils, brass, pewter, bedding, and all other my substance whatsoever". The total value amounted to £42.95p, perhaps more than £500 of our money today. It appeared, also, that he owned the modest dwelling in St Cuthbert's parish where he lived.

At the end of 1688 *The Acceptable Sacrifice* was published with a preface by George Cokayn. Among John's papers Elizabeth found a number of unpublished manuscripts which he had prepared for the press. But how to proceed with them? On the advice of one of his publishers, Nathaniel Ponder, she inserted an advertisement in the *Mercurius Reformatus*, one of the newspapers of the time: "Mr John Bunyan, Author of *The Pilgrim's Progress* and many other excellent books, that have found great acceptance, hath left behind him ten manuscripts prepared by himself for the press before his death: his Widow is desired to print them ... which will make a book for 10 shillings, in sheets, in folio. All persons who desire so great and good a work should be performed with speed, are desired to send in five shillings for their first payment to Norman Newman at the King's Arms in the Poultrey, London."

This notice caught the eager eye of Charles Doe, who proceeded post-haste to Bedford and interviewed Elizabeth and studied the manuscripts. A deal was soon made and so, devoted follower of John Bunyan as he was, Charles Doe became a publisher as well as a comb-maker. In his Folio of 1692 Doe published twelve of the manuscripts, previously mentioned, and in 1698 *The Heavenly Footman*. In all he sold about 3,000 of Bunyan's books.

Elizabeth lived on in the little house in Bedford where she died in 1691, loved and honoured by all. Like her John's Christiana, she no doubt called for some Bedford Great-heart and Valiant-for-truth, to whom she commended her children for their spiritual care. "The last word she was heard to say was, 'I come, Lord, to be with Thee and bless thee'. "... So she went and called, and entered in at the Gate with all the ceremonies of joy that her husband Christian had done before her."

13

The Man

1

Dr Alexander Whyte, a great lover and student of John Bunyan, whose lectures on Bunyan Characters are so spiritually penetrating and strengthening, has this to say about character in his first volume. "Character comes up out of the heart. There are more good minds in the world than there are good hearts. There are more clever people than good people; character, high, spotless, saintly character, is a far rarer thing in this world than talent or even genius. And yet so true is it that the world loves its own, that all men worship talent, and even bodily strength and bodily beauty, while only one here and one there either understands or values or pursues moral character, though it is the strength and the beauty and the sweetness of the soul."

Bunyan would have endorsed that. He had come into contact with many men better educated and more cultured than he, but he had found them false, insincere and time-serving. He, as he tells us, "never went to school to Plato or Aristotle", but he had been led to the Cross, and spent the rest of his days in the school of Christ. He is at one and the same time Mr. Greatheart, Mr. Standfast, and Mr. Valiant-for-truth. But it is possible to see some of the strands that were woven into his character to make him the man and the genius he was.

There was first and foremost in John Bunyan a deep personal love for his Saviour, the Lord Jesus Christ. "O methought, Christ! Christ! There was nothing but Christ that was now before my eyes!" And again, "Twas glorious to me to see His exaltation, and the worth and prevalency of all His benefits. And that because I could now look from myself to Him, and should reckon that all those graces of God that were now green on me, were yet but like those crack-groats and four-pence-half-pennies that rich men carry in their purses, when their gold is in their trunks at home! O, I saw that my gold was all in my trunk at home! Even in Christ, my Lord and my Saviour! Now Christ was my all! He was made of God to me all my Wisdom, all my Righteousness, all my Sanctification, and all my Redemption!" And yet again: "Where-ever I have seen the print of His shoe in the earth, there I have coveted to set my foot too." Bunyan's books are full of Christ—his welcome, his saving grace, his unshakeable truth, his advocacy for sinners, and so on. We can forgive him for his occasional lapses from good taste, and his over-emphasis sometimes on divine judgement, for the sake of his personal devotion to his Saviour, and the way in which he warms our hearts towards Christ. His preaching and writing were Christ-centred, and it was this that carried men's hearts captive to Christ. If our present-day preachers and theologians had the same emphasis a very different spirit would prevail in both the Church and the State.

2

Bunyan held the vital elements of the Puritan faith with the utmost constancy. The Protestant emphasis on the authority and sufficiency of the Scriptures concerning Christian doctrine and life was basic with him as with all Puritans. "I prefer the Bible, and having that still with me, I count myself far better furnished than if I had without it all the libraries of the two universities.' The Sovereignty of God in creation, providence, and redemption was also, a matter of deep conviction. The desire to know and do God's will and to please him, even in the smallest things, made the Puritans take a high and serious view of human life and destiny, and kept their consciences under the control of the Holy Spirit. They were men who walked with God and were actuated first and always by moral and spiritual considerations, and not merely by materialistic or economic or political notions. In all these ways John Bunyan held the Puritan view and was moulded by it.

And thus he came to a spiritual mind. The Bible, prayer, worship, Christian fellowship, Puritan writings, wrought in him a spiritual outlook and emphasis. It was not for nothing that the Puritans were called "the godly". The instructed Puritan found his authority in the Spirit-prompted response of his heart and mind to the Word. So it is that when Christian meets on the road to the Celestial City people such as Pliable, Mr. Wordly-wiseman, Formalist, Hypocrisy, Talkative, Judge Hategood his attitude to them, and his advice to them is born of Bunyan's knowledge of spiritual things and his understanding of the teaching of the Bible. Dr. John Owen, a Puritan divine of great spirituality of mind as his great books show, delighted to listen to John Bunyan for this very reason, that the mind of the Lord was in and behind all the preaching. By grace he was a new man in Christ, and his writing and preaching carry the fragrance of it.

There was in Bunyan, also, a deep-rooted tenacity of purpose, a manliness, a trait of character that would never yield once he was convinced his purpose was right. "Set your face like a flint," urged Evangelist, and Bunyan did just that. He was no Pliable or Facing-both-ways. He did not endure twelve years of imprisonment for a whim or a fancy. It was the witness of his conscience against the carnal reasonings and legislation of ungodly men, his testimony to his call to preach God's Word come what may. "I am at a point with you," he declared boldly to Kelynge. "If I was out of prison today, I would preach the Gospel again tomorrow, by the help of God.'' This is British courage sanctified! And it has served the nation well in many ages and many causes.

There is also in Bunyan a homeliness that is very attractive. He was very happy in his homelife, when not in prison, enjoying the simple things of family life, playing with the children and making toys for them. In *Pilgrim's Progress* and other books he refers to everyday things and activities as one accustomed to them. In the Interpreter's House, for example, are the candle, the broom, the sprinkled water, the two children each in his little chair, the fire burning, the vessel of oil, the main with the inkhorn. Each homely thing brings some spiritual lesson, and so all along the pilgrim way. He is never high-flown in his descriptions. And the simple, enduring qualities in people—affection, sympathy, helpfulness, courage are what he delights in and points out to us. He had them abundantly in himself.

3

His imagination was of the highest order. When he described the Slough of Despond, the fight with Apollyon, Doubting Castle and its Giant, he makes us see and thrill and grasp it all. Here are states of experience visualized to completeness. A few phrases, and men and places are before our eyes. Giant Despair has a grim and surly voice; his dungeon is nasty and stinking; his wife urges him to beat the pilgrims, which he does; and he himself has fainting fits; the remembered key of Promise lets the pillgrims go free. Vanity Fair is full of bustle and splendour like London on Lord Mayor's Day, as Lord Macaulay says, but also with thefts, murders, adulteries, and many other hurtful things open or concealed. This, and the trial of the pilgrims is one of the master-pieces of Bunyan's inventive faculty.

John Bunyan's literary style is of the very finest English. It is clear, plain, directly expressed. Coleridge, no mean judge, spoke of "the inimitable *Pilgrim's Progress*, that model of beautiful, pure, and harmonious English." Dr Samuel

Johnson praised John Bunyan highly, and *The Pilgrim's Progress* was one of the few books he liked to re-read. "His *Pilgrim's Progress*", he observed, "has great merit, both for invention, imagination, and the conduct of the story; and it has the best evidence of its merit, the general and continued approbation of mankind!" Bunyan's style is recommended by Lord Macaulay as "an invaluable study to every person who wishes to gain a wide command over the English language. Its vocabulary is the vocabulary of the common people." Bunyan's perfect English style was wrought by constant reading of the English Bible. Robert Browning in his poem, "Ned Bratts", makes Ned say,

> His language was not ours:
> 'Tis my belief, God spake;
> No tinker has such powers.

Bunyan was not unconcerned about the social problems of his day. In his *Christian Behaviour* he writes of "moral duties Gospelized." Masters must not forget that they have duties both to the bodies and souls of their servants. They must beware of turning them into slaves by overworking or underpaying them, by beguiling them with false promises and "wire-drawing" them to "such wages as indeed is too little and inconsiderable for such work." He goes on, "I have heard some poor servants say that in some carnal families they have had more liberty to God's things, and more fairness of dealing, than among professors. But this stinketh." "Servants are goers as well as comers; take heed that thou give them no occasion to scandal the Gospel when they are gone, for what they observed thee unrighteously to do when they were with thee." In his *Badman* he urges that in commercial dealings a man should design his neighbour's good and profit as his own, and the theory that a man has the right to buy in the cheapest market and sell in the dearest is dismissed as contrary to the New Testament. "Every man that makes a prey of his advantage upon his neighbour's necessities to force upon him more than in reason and conscience, such commodity is worth, may very well be called an extortioner, and judged for one that hath no inheritance in the Kingdom of Heaven.." And he is indignant with those who rig the market, crying, "Scarcity! Scarcity!" where there is none. Neither has he any mercy for extortionate money-lenders: "Such miscreants are the pest and vermin of the Commonwealth, not fit for the society of men." He anticipates that some may criticize him for not sticking to the simple Gospel. "Perhaps some folk will find fault with me for my meddling with other folks' matters, and for thus prying into the secrets of their iniquity. But to such I would say, since such actions are evil, it is time they were hissed out of the world." The greatest need in England, he goes on to say, is a thorough New Testament reformation from the soul outward.

In his book, *The Jerusalem Sinner Saved*, in which he refers to Martha and Mary, he has something to say about women's attire. One of the first acts of the converted Mary was to change her gay and wanton attire for a modest dress. The Restoration pride of dress, both in man and woman, exercised him greatly. What, he would know, can be the end of those that are so fond of decking themselves in this antic manner? Why are folk going about nowadays with their bull's foretops and naked shoulders and painted faces? Even some Puritans decked themselves in a "spangling show". "For my own part, I have seen many myself, and those church members too, so decked and bedaubed with their fangles and toys, and that when they have been at the solemn appointments of God in the way of his worship, that I have wondered with what face such painted persons could sit in the place where they were without swooning". He recalls that he once took it upon him to "talk with a maid by way of reproof for her fond and gaudy garment. But she told me the tailor would make it so, when alas! poor, proud girl, she gave order to the tailor to so make it."

And he is not very happy about the condition of the Dissenting churches under the Restoration. It was "a day that was never heard of, wherein conversion is frequent without repentance", so that churches "swarm with them that religiously name the name of Christ but yet depart not from iniquity" (*A Holy Life*). At the same time he is against the extreme narrowness of some his fellow Puritans. The saints, he complains, are often so unloveable, "they will mix their mercies with so many twits," whereas God gives without twitting. "Why not familiar with sinners, provided we hate their spots and blemishes and seek that they may be healed of them? Why not fellowly with our carnal neighbours" if we use the occasion to seek their good?

4

He has something to say about Christian unity in his book, *The Holy City*, a subject which much exercises Christians today. The grace and power of the true Church, he says, comes from above, just as in The Revelation the Holy City descends from above. The New Jerusalem is the spiritual society of the faithful. "It shall not be then, as now, a Popish doctrine, a Quaker's doctrine, a Prelatical doctrine, and the Presbyter, Independent and Anabaptist, thus distinguished, and thus confounded and destroying." There shall be an undivided fellowship ruled by love. It marks will be holiness, goodness, and truth. Its glory is spiritual and heavenly, not worldly. Bunyan's tolerance and large-heartedness are unmistakeable. "Not only is there no fanaticism," says Goldwin Smith, "but there is hardly even anything sectarian in his writings. Saving one or two passages about the Pope, they might almost have been used by Francis of Assisi, to whose spiritual character that of Bunyan has a certain affinity." The name he would be known by is that of Christian. He challenged the whole separatist position centred, as it was, on ritual ordinances such as baptism, which he denied was of the essence of the Gospel. "I count them not the fundamentals of our Christianity." The rule to gather men into Church communion is the rule of faith in Christ, and moral duties Gospelized. "For God's people to divide into parties or to shut each other from Church communion hath heretofore (i.e. in the New Testament) been counted carnal and the actors herein babyish Christians."

5

John Bunyan's books, especially *The Pilgrim's Progress*, had a large circulation in his day, the great Allegory alone reaching a sale of 100,000 copies during the last decade of his life. Edition followed edition in the centuries to come, and translation after translation into many languages.. In the New England colonies of America also, Bunyan's Pilgrim was known and loved, as Bunyan remarks in his rhymed Introduction to Part Two:

'Tis in New England under such advance,
Receives there so much loving Countenance
As to be Trim'd, new Cloth'd and decked with gems,
That it might show its features and its limbs,
Yet more; so comely doth my Pilgrim walk,
That of him thousands daily sing and talk.

Coleridge wrote on the fly-leaf of his copy of *The Pilgrim's Progress*, "I know of no book, the Bible excepted as above all comparison, which I, according to my judgement and experience, could so safely recommend as teaching and enforcing the whole saving truth according to the mind that was in Christ Jesus, as *The Pilgrim's Progress*."

And it is this, his pointing to Christ and his truth and salvation, rather than his stand for religious liberty, great as that was, which is his chief message to our day and age. He tells us that as he was visited and laid hold of and transformed by the abounding grace of the Lord Jesus Christ, so we may be, and so we too may know what life is in the Spirit, and the light and joy and peace which only Christ can give. So also may we negotiate all the hazards of the Pilgrim way with divine strength and guidance, and enter with rejoicing into the Celestial City.

"Bunyan", remarks Gwilym O. Griffith, "hardly less than

any other living man, helped to keep the soul of England alive.'' This is a noble tribute and a just one, and one to confer immortality upon him. He is still at work upon those who read him and partake of his spirit.

Select Bibliography

Major works of John Bunyan:

Grace Abounding to the Chief of Sinners (1666)

The Pilgrim's Progress

Part One (1678)

Part Two (1685)

The Life and Death of Mr Badman (1680)

The Holy War (1682)

Other books:

Maurice Ashley: *The English Civil War*

Maurice Ashley: *The Greatness of Oliver Cromwell*

G.F. Barbour: *Life of Alexander Whyte*

Henry Bettensen (ed.): *Documents of the Christian Church*

Vera Brittain: *In the Steps of John Bunyan*

John Brown: *John Bunyan, his Life, Times and Work*

D.R. Davies: *In Search of Myself*

John Drinkwater: *Cromwell, a Character Study*

Sir Charles Firth: *Oliver Cromwell*

Sir Charles Firth: *Essays Historical and Literary*

J.R. Green: *Short History of the English People*

Gwilym O. Griffith: *John Bunyan*

Charles G. Harper: *The Bunyan Country*

F. Mott Harrison: *John Bunyan*

G.B. Harrison: *John Bunyan, a Study in Personality*

Florence Higham: *Faith of Our Fathers*

Hugh Martin: *Puritanism and Richard Baxter*

R.S. Paul: The Religion of Oliver Cromwell

R. Sharrock: *John Bunyan*

Skeats & Miall: *History of the Free Churches*

Gilbert Thomas: *Autobiography, 1891 to 1941*

Gilbert Thomas: *Builders and Makers*

G.M. Trevelyan: *History of England*

G.M. Trevelyan: *England Under the Stuarts*

J. Tucker & L.S. Winstock: *The English Civil War: a Military Handbook*

Alexander Whyte: *Bunyan Characters* (4 volumes)